INVITATION TO
THE NEW TESTAMENT
EPISTLES II

INVITATION TO
THE NEW TESTAMENT
EPISTLES II

This volume continues a series of commentaries on the books of the Bible, specially designed to answer the need for a lively, contemporary guide to the written Word. Here is the best of contemporary biblical scholarship, together with the world-renowned *Jerusalem Bible* text. In addition, there are study questions that will provoke and inspire further discussion.

The Pauline Epistles have traditionally been considered as letters from the great Apostle to the Gentiles to the churches he founded or to his trusted co-workers. They serve to warn of trouble, to correct problems, to instruct in the faith, to refresh a troubled or flagging spirit—in short, to remind the Church of the reality of God in their lives.

In his letters to the Thessalonians and Corinthians, Paul addresses new Christian communities whose initial excitement with the gospel is increasingly threatened by the realities of life. Paul exhorts these new churches to accept these problems as part of Christianity.

Unlike the Thessalonians and the Corinthians, the Philippians were always dedicated to the gospel and loved and accepted Paul. This epistle is a firm but warm exhortation to accept thoroughly the challenge of Christian heroism.

The letter to Philemon is the shortest and most personal of the Pauline epistles. Written to persuade Philemon to take back a runaway slave, the letter exhibits Paul's use of rhetoric and psychology in the service of the gospel.

Just as he spoke to the Christians of his day, Paul speaks to today's followers of Christ. The problems he wrote about are still found in today's world and studying these Epistles can be of help, solace and inspiration.

INVITATION TO THE NEW TESTAMENT EPISTLES II presents these Epistles and their message in a format that can be easily used for individual study, daily meditation and/or group discussion. It is an indispensable volume for any Christian library.

INVITATION TO THE NEW TESTAMENT EPISTLES II

A Commentary on 1 Thessalonians, 2 Thessalonians, 1 Corinthians, 2 Corinthians, Philippians, and Philemon with Complete Text from The Jerusalem Bible

EUGENE A. LAVERDIERE

IMAGE BOOKS
A Division of Doubleday & Company, Inc.
Garden City, New York
1980

ISBN: 0-385-14797-X
Library of Congress Catalog Card Number: 79-7788

To My Sister Claudette
A Woman of Maryknoll

CONTENTS

ABBREVIATIONS OF THE BOOKS
OF THE BIBLE

Ac	Acts	Lk	Luke
Am	Amos	Lm	Lamentations
Ba	Baruch	Lv	Leviticus
1 Ch	1 Chronicles	1 M	1 Maccabees
2 Ch	2 Chronicles	2 M	2 Maccabees
1 Co	1 Corinthians	Mi	Micah
2 Co	2 Corinthians	Mk	Mark
Col	Colossians	Ml	Malachi
Dn	Daniel	Mt	Matthew
Dt	Deuteronomy	Na	Nahum
Ep	Ephesians	Nb	Numbers
Est	Esther	Ne	Nehemiah
Ex	Exodus	Ob	Obadiah
Ezk	Ezekiel	1 P	1 Peter
Ezr	Ezra	2 P	2 Peter
Ga	Galatians	Ph	Philippians
Gn	Genesis	Phm	Philemon
Hab	Habakkuk	Pr	Proverbs
Heb	Hebrews	Ps	Psalms
Hg	Haggai	Qo	Ecclesiastes
Ho	Hosea	Rm	Romans
Is	Isaiah	Rt	Ruth
Jb	Job	Rv	Revelation
Jdt	Judith	1 S	1 Samuel
Jg	Judges	2 S	2 Samuel
Jl	Joel	Sg	Song of Songs
Jm	James	Si	Ecclesiasticus
Jn	John	Tb	Tobit
1 Jn	1 John	1 Th	1 Thessalonians
2 Jn	2 John	2 Th	2 Thessalonians
3 Jn	3 John	1 Tm	1 Timothy
Jon	Jonah	2 Tm	2 Timothy
Jos	Joshua	Tt	Titus
Jr	Jeremiah	Ws	Wisdom
Jude	Jude	Zc	Zechariah
1 K	1 Kings	Zp	Zephaniah
2 K	2 Kings		

GENERAL INTRODUCTION TO THE DOUBLEDAY NEW TESTAMENT COMMENTARY SERIES

Let me introduce this new commentary series on the New Testament by sharing some experiences. In my job as New Testament Book Review Editor for the *Catholic Biblical Quarterly,* scores of books pass through my hands each year. As I evaluate these books and send them out to reviewers, I cannot help but think that so little of this scholarly research will make its way into the hands of the educated lay person.

In talking at biblical institutes and to charismatic and lay study groups, I find an almost unquenchable thirst for the Word of God. People want to learn more; they want to study. But when they ask me to recommend commentaries on the New Testament, I'm stumped. What commentaries can I put into their hands, commentaries that do not have the technical jargon of scholars and that really communicate to the educated laity?

The goal of this popular commentary series is to make the best of contemporary scholarship available to the educated lay person in a highly readable and understandable way. The commentaries avoid footnotes and other scholarly apparatus. They are short and sweet. The authors make their points in a clear way and don't fatigue their readers with unnecessary detail.

Another outstanding feature of this commentary series is that it is based on The Jerusalem Bible translation, which is serialized with the commentary. This lively and easily understandable translation has received rave reviews from millions of readers. It is the interstate of translations and avoids the stoplights of local-road translations.

A signal feature of the commentaries on the Gospels is that they explore the way each evangelist used the sayings and deeds of Jesus to meet the needs of his church. The commentators answer the question: How did each evangelist guide, challenge, teach, and console the members of his community with the message of Jesus? The commentators are not interested in the evangelist's message for its own sake, but explain that message with one eye on present application.

This last-mentioned feature goes hand and glove with the innovative feature of appending Study Questions to the explanations of individual passages. By means of these Study Questions the commentator moves from an explanation of the message of the evangelist to a consideration of how this message might apply to believers today.

Each commentator has two highly important qualifications: scholarly expertise and the proven ability to communicate the results of solid scholarship to the people of God.

I am confident that this new commentary series will meet a real need as it helps people to unlock a door to the storehouse of God's Word where they will find food for life.

ROBERT J. KARRIS, O.F.M.
Associate Professor of New Testament Studies,
Catholic Theological Union and
Chicago Cluster of Theological Schools

INTRODUCTION

Christian history has had many heroes, figures who dominated their world and epitomized the challenge of Christ. One of these heroes was Paul, a Christian Jew who reached out to the Gentiles of the mid-first century and made an enormous contribution to the development and universalization of Christianity.

In the course of his work, Paul wrote a number of letters which are now included in the New Testament, and among these we find two to the church of Thessalonika, two to that of Corinth, one to the Philippians and a brief personal letter to Philemon, a leading Christian at Colossae. These letters, which span a little over a decade of Paul's apostolic life (A.D. 51 to 62), are included in the present volume along with a brief commentary, inviting all to join Paul in his vision of life and his mission to Christianity and to the world.

In order to accept this invitation profitably, however, we must have a clear sense of the nature of Paul's spirit and work, of the experience and understanding which drove him in the service of the Gospel, as well as of the role which the letters played in his apostolic and pastoral efforts. Such are the subjects of this introduction.

Paul was essentially and eminently an apostolic person intent on bearing the good news of God to the farthest regions of the Greco-Roman world. Christ had appeared to him (1 Co 15:8) and filled him with a vision of God's kingdom (1 Co 15:24–28), calling him to join Christ in glory and impelling him to reach out to all human beings with the good news he had received.

The good news bore on the full potential of human life which God realized and manifested in the person of Jesus Christ the risen Lord. All who turned to Christ were empowered by God's Spirit to share in his life and fulfill their deepest yearning to transcend the temporal boundaries of earthly life. To do so, their present life had to be patterned on that of Christ who fully accepted the limitations of humanity and especially the most radical of those limitations: death (Ph 2:6–11).

Reduced to its simplest statement, Paul's gospel word was thus the very Cross of Christ (1 Co 1:17–18). Through the Cross, Christ burst into glory as the first of all who accepted to follow him (1 Co 15:23). Accordingly, any Christian teaching which ignores the Cross or does not include the Cross as its foundation is a betrayal of the Christian message.

The Cross of Christ provides the basic pattern for understanding and accepting sufferings, difficulties, persecutions and death itself in a life bent on the salvation of others. The paradox of Christ's death-resurrection is thus the basic paradox of every Christian life. Gifted by God's self-communication in Christ, Christians are justified in their faith response (Rm 5:1). In baptism, that response is affirmed as a willingness to die and to be buried with Christ (Rm 6:3–4). Having received a share in the life of Christ, who already is risen, the Christian lives according to his or her commitment and progressively follows on the way to salvation and fullness of life with the risen Lord (Rm 6:4).

As Paul made his way through the Greco-Roman world, all who accepted his Gospel message of salvation and entered into his vision of life joined in communities. Such communities arose at Thessalonika,

Corinth and Ephesus, all three of which were major cities and centers of culture and commerce along the seaways and highways of Rome's vast communication network. As the capital cities of Macedonia, Achaia and Asia, they were also centers of administration in an empire which included all the lands bordering on the Mediterranean.

Brought to centers such as these, Christianity radiated in centripetal fashion throughout their respective provinces and beyond. Paul had wisely devoted much of his apostolic effort to these three cities, along with Philippi, an inland Roman colony in eastern Macedonia, and Troas, an important port and the point of embarkation for Neapolis, the port of Philippi, from which one traveled along the Via Egnatia to Thessalonika.

Once planted, the Christian word had to be nurtured. Unable to be everywhere, it was still essential that the young plants be watered. While others could surely do this work, Paul could hardly abandon the communities which he had fathered through God's Gospel word. When difficulties arose, he consequently made every effort to pay a return visit. Paul's apostolic work of evangelization thus flowed quite naturally into the pastoral care of those who had responded to his challenge. Paul's return visits and travel plans play an important role in his correspondence, and their significance cannot be overestimated.

Paul viewed Christian communication first and foremost as a matter of personal presence and the spoken word. The reason for this is profoundly theological. The living Lord was encountered in the person and word of his followers, and the process of salvation was facilitated in the sharing which characterized their assembly. The transmission and development of Christianity, whose ramifications affected every aspect of personal and social life, was thus realized through the imitation of those who had already heard the gospel and faithfully maintained their commitment to it. It is in this interpersonal context that tradition was both handed down and applied to new situations and challenges.

Paul's principle of imitation is clearly a key component of Christian life in history. Without it, tradition would have been reduced to mere words, unrelated to the life experiences which they were meant to articulate.

Pressing needs in one apostolic arena did not always allow Paul to leave his work, and at times persecutions or internal difficulties rendered a Pauline visit unfeasible or inopportune. In these circumstances, Paul would normally send a co-worker in his place. Timothy, for example, and Titus were entrusted with such missions. Both of these men shared Paul's vision and life. In his absence, they were able to represent his person and efforts, and their word and decisions could be accepted as those of Paul himself.

This alternate and indirect manner of communication, however, did not satisfy Paul's apostolic and pastoral need to be with the communities. Accordingly, he turned to letter writing. With the help of a secretary, he wrote the letters which are now in the New Testament as well as a number of others, which he then entrusted to a close colleague or to a representative of the community being addressed. The letters were thus intended as a temporary substitute for a personal visit. They went a long way toward overcoming the distance which separated Paul from those he loved. Neither the visit of others, however, nor the letters could be expected to fully replace Paul's personal presence. Using the letters to prepare his coming, Paul frequently expresses his desire to visit the community as soon as possible.

In writing these letters, Paul never loses sight of the context of the assembly in which they were to be read. They are thus filled with liturgical formulas as well as references to prayer and worship. These formulas are particularly prominent in the greetings which frame the body of each letter. The letters also include long passages reminiscent of Paul's apostolic and homiletic discourses. Destined for public reading, their style remains close to Paul's own spoken word.

Ever conscious of the living word which had been planted, Paul repeatedly refers to his activity, way of life and teaching during his previous stay or visit with a community. Once shared, his word lived in the tradition which had been received and integrated in the community's life. It thus provided Paul with a point of departure for discussion and for resolving problems. Accordingly, while Paul is open to new developments, he is always sensitive to continuity and consistency with tradition. It is in this interest, for example, that he cites liturgical and creedal formulas (1 Co 11:23–25, 15:3–5) as well as an important Christian hymn (Ph 2:6–11).

Over nineteen hundred years later, Paul's letters are still being read in the Christian assembly. Paul's original co-workers have been replaced by large numbers of Christians, the Timothys and Tituses of our own age, men and women commissioned to extend Paul's presence not only across the miles which separate communities geographically but also across the years and centuries which prevent Paul from being present in the flesh.

Bonded to Paul in the body of Christ, these Chris-

tians again echo his fidelity to tradition and wrestle
with new situations and problems. To do so faithfully
and effectively, however, they must be imitators of Paul
as he had been of Christ. Like Paul these ministers are
but earthen vessels, but for all their fragility Christ
truly lives in them as he had lived in Paul. Paul's word
thus continues to be grounded in experience and in
lives which have taken the Cross seriously in the service of Christ's Gospel. It is in this spirit that we are invited to take up Paul's word and make it our own.

Modern printing and publication, however, have introduced a new factor which places the record of Paul's
message in the hands of all. The letters can thus be
read outside the assembly and be an important source
of prayer, reflection and study. All are thus invited to
pore over the words of Paul, this minister of the new
covenant in the early moments which followed its birth.
Challenged by his efforts, we work for the full estab-
lishment of the Kingdom and for the day when God
will be all in all.

INVITATION TO
THE NEW TESTAMENT
EPISTLES II

1 Thessalonians
The First Letter of Paul
to the Church in Thessalonika

INTRODUCTION

Paul's first letter to the church of the Thessalonians is the oldest piece of writing in the New Testament and the oldest work of Christian literature. However, it was not intended as literature, and Paul would doubtless be astounded at the worldwide interest granted to this personal missive, which he wrote from Corinth toward the end of the year 51 to a fledgling community in the Macedonian capital.

No one who reads the letter at one sitting will fail to sense the exuberance which pervades the entire letter. Although it was written rapidly and with little thought to style, the letter betrays a disciplined sense of order, freedom of movement, intensity of expression and a driving need to communicate. The written word did not dull the apostolic voice of one who spared no effort to speak the Gospel fearlessly, selflessly and to all. Such is the "stuff" of great literature.

Breaking through existing patterns of expression, Paul created a new literary form, the Christian apostolic letter, a form related but not reducible to the Greek and Jewish forms of ancient letter writing. Forged in the fire of Christian experience and shaped on the anvil of Gospel proclamation, the Christian apostolic letter stands unique in the world of literary communication.

In reading the letter, we are invited to join a community with but a few months of Christian experience. We are called to share its initial excitement as well as the troubling events which threatened its commitment but which proved essential to its growth and development. The community's problems, which include resistance to the universal mission, maintaining holiness of life, the needless dependence of some on the charity of others, the meaning of death, and the return of Christ, are ours as well.

We are also invited to join Paul, Silvanus and Timothy as they address the community (1:1), discuss vital issues which place its conversion in historical and religious perspective (1:2–3:13), urge all the members to steadfastness in holiness, love and faith (4:1–5:22), and ask for prayers in return for their own (5:23–28). The apostles' sense of zealous responsibility for those with whom they have shared the Gospel of Christ should be infectious.

In order to respond to this invitation, we should view our own Christian efforts as ever young and ever beginning. Like Thessalonians, we are challenged to imitate those who have transmitted God's life to us, to become worthy of imitation and be a source of life for others. The Thessalonian community will thus mirror our own hesitation, internal difficulties and external conflicts, and Paul's letter will help to direct our steps in the Christian way of faith, love and hope.

1 Thessalonians 1:1
GRACE AND PEACE

¹ **1** From Paul, Silvanus and Timothy, to the Church in Thessalonika which is in God the Father and the Lord Jesus Christ; wishing you grace and peace.

✠

The first letter to the church in Thessalonika opens with a form of address (1:1) which would be characteristic of all the Pauline letters. The elements of this form include the name of the sender, the addressee and a greeting.

As in the second letter to the same church, Paul introduces himself as the first of three senders. Silvanus and Timothy, Paul's associates in what proved to be a long and difficult missionary venture, had recently joined Paul at Corinth, and their names are included as co-senders. From the letter's concluding verses, however, which use the first person singular in place of the plural (5:25,27), Paul is clearly seen as the letter's principal sender.

The addressee is the church in Thessalonika and not the members of that church taken individually. Paul thus has a strong sense of the community in which those who heard his message are now bonded. That bond consists in a common relationship to God the Father and to the Lord Jesus Christ, as is clearly in-

dicated by the theological expressions which define the
church in Thessalonika.

The greeting is a prayerful wish that the church receive grace and peace, that is the full blessing of the
covenant from the point of view of its source (grace)
and its results (peace). Since these are to be granted by
the Father and the Lord Jesus Christ, in whom the
church's very existence is grounded, the covenant blessing transcends the old covenant and consists in the new
Christian covenant which fulfills it.

STUDY QUESTIONS: What are the basic elements in the
                 address of the Pauline apostolic
                 letter? What is the theological sig-
                 nificance of the greeting formula?

1 Thessalonians 1:2–10
UNDYING GRATITUDE

² We always mention you in our prayers and
³ thank God for you all, ·and constantly remember
before God our Father how you have shown your
faith in action, worked for love and persevered
through hope, in our Lord Jesus Christ.
⁴ We know, brothers, that God loves you and
⁵ that you have been chosen, ·because when we
brought the Good News to you, it came to you
not only as words, but as power and as the Holy
Spirit and as utter conviction. And you observed
the sort of life we lived when we were with you,
⁶ which was for your instruction, ·and you were led
to become imitators of us, and of the Lord; and
it was with the joy of the Holy Spirit that you took
to the gospel, in spite of the great opposition all
⁷ around you. ·This has made you the great exam-
ple to all believers in Macedonia and Achaia
⁸ since it was from you that the word of the Lord
started to spread—and not only throughout Macedonia and Achaia, for the news of your faith in
God has spread everywhere. We do not need to
⁹ tell other people about it: ·other people tell us
how we started the work among you, how you
broke with idolatry when you were converted to
God and became servants of the real, living God;
¹⁰ and how you are now waiting for Jesus, his Son,
whom he raised from the dead, to come from
heaven to save us from the retribution which is
coming.

✠

As happens in all of Paul's letters save Galatians, the author then turns to prayerful sentiments of thanksgiving. In this first letter, however, this does not stand out as a formal unit but as the dominant theme and the subject of the entire first part of the letter (1:2–3:13).

Paul had precipitously left Thessalonika in the wake of turbulence occasioned by his preaching of the Gospel message. Timothy's return with the good news from that city had now calmed Paul's anxiety over the church's welfare and released the exuberant gratitude which he shares with the Thessalonian church and all who would one day read his letter.

In 1:2–10, we have a general statement concerning Paul's constant prayer of thanksgiving. The passage focuses on the church's origins in the recent past and on how it now stands poised for the expected future return of God's Son. This triple movement from the past to the present and to the future, which is associated with the dynamic relationship of faith to charity and to hope, would describe the basic literary movement of formal thanksgiving units in the later letters.

The order in which faith, charity and hope are presented in 1:2–3, reflects a basic element in Paul's Christian psychology, according to which charity is the expression of faith, and hope is grounded in both faith and charity. His allusion to the constancy of hope reflects the recent threat to the church's continued existence. Note that all three of these basic elements in the Christian attitude are credited not to the community's own resources but to the work of our Lord Jesus Christ.

Paul then presents the concrete historical grounds for the previous assertions (1:4–10). Readdressing the readers as brothers who are beloved of God, he affirms that they are God's elect. This he knows for certain because the Gospel he presented to them moved beyond mere words to powerful works which are expressions of the Holy Spirit. The Thessalonians share the same knowledge of how Paul and his colleagues had evangelized them. They had in turn imitated this service and become a model for all believers in Macedonia and Achaia. In their imitation of Paul, they had become imitators of the Lord himself.

As a result, all know how they had been converted to God and now await his Son Jesus, whom God had raised from the dead and who would deliver us from the wrath to come. These verses highlight an extremely important aspect of Paul's view of continuity in the life of the church. Christians are called to imitate those who evangelize them that they too might be imitated by others.

STUDY QUESTIONS: What is the immediate occasion for the writing of 1 Thessalonians? What is the principle which governs the order and movement of Paul's thanksgiving units? How is this principle related to faith, charity and hope? What is the basic principle of continuity in Christian history and tradition?

1 Thessalonians 2:1–12
PAUL AT THESSALONIKA

¹ 2 You know yourselves, my brothers, that our visit to you has not proved ineffectual. ² We had, as you know, been given rough treatment and been grossly insulted at Philippi, and it was our God who gave us the courage to proclaim his Good News to you in the face of great opposition. ·³ We have not taken to preaching because we are deluded or immoral or trying to deceive anyone; ·⁴ it was God who decided that we were fit to be entrusted with the Good News, and when we are speaking, we are not trying to please men but ⁵ God, who can read our inmost thoughts. ·You know very well, and we can swear it before God, that never at any time have our speeches been simply flattery or a cover for trying to get money; ⁶ nor have we ever looked for any special honor ⁷ from men, either from you or anybody else, ·when we could have imposed ourselves on you with full weight, as apostles of Christ.

Instead, we were unassuming. Like a mother ⁸ feeding and looking after her own children, ·we felt so devoted and protective toward you, and had come to love you so much, that we were eager to hand over to you not only the Good News ⁹ but our whole lives as well. ·Let me remind you, brothers, how hard we used to work, slaving night and day so as not to be a burden on any one of you while we were proclaiming God's Good News ¹⁰ to you. ·You are witnesses, and so is God, that our treatment of you, since you became believers, ¹¹ has been impeccably right and fair. ·You can remember how we treated every one of you as a ¹² father treats his children, ·teaching you what was

right, encouraging you and appealing to you to
live a life worthy of God, who is calling you to
share the glory of his kingdom.

✠

After the general statement concerning the grounds
for grateful prayer (1:2–10), the letter goes over the
same reflections in detail. In 2:1–12, Paul begins by
recalling his own recent experience, first at Philippi
where he had suffered insults. God, however, had not
allowed the latter to impede Paul's confident preaching
at Thessalonika in the midst of further conflict
(2:2–3).

Already tested by God, Paul had presented the Gospel entrusted to him without regard for pleasing his
auditors. Since flattery, cupidity and human glory
played no part in his efforts he had been able truly to
be an apostle, bringing to bear the full and unadul-
terated weight of his apostleship (2:4–7a).

Pursuing this extraordinary personal and value-laden
autobiography, Paul recalls how he had made himself
small in their midst. Like a mother for her children, his
tenderness had expressed willingness to give his own
life, even as he gave them the Gospel of God. The
Christians of Thessalonika are witnesses also to the
way he had been like a father to them, urging them to
live a life worthy of God who calls them to his glorious
kingdom (2:7b–12).

These statements of solidarity in the communication
of the Gospel develop the principle of imitation
(1:4–10) in terms of the giving of life, an ongoing
effort which begins with the Gospel's initial proclamation and which continues with the apostle's develop-

ment of the Gospel's implications. Imitation is thus
based on the actual transmission of life. Paul's efforts
are comparable to the role of a mother and a father,
who set all self-interest aside as they nurture their children. In the midst of difficulties, he envisages even the
threat of death as of no consequence. In sharing the
Gospel, an apostle must be willing even to lay down his
life that others might live.

STUDY QUESTIONS: What metaphors does Paul use to
                 express his relationship to the
                 Christian community? How are
                 these related to the principle of
                 imitation?

1 Thessalonians 2:13–16
THE RESPONSE OF THE THESSALONIANS

13   Another reason why we constantly thank God for you is that as soon as you heard the message that we brought you as God's message, you accepted it for what it really is, God's message and not some human thinking; and it is still a living
14 power among you who believe it. ·For you, my brothers, have been like the churches of God in Christ Jesus which are in Judaea, in suffering the same treatment from your own countrymen as
15 they have suffered from the Jews, ·the people who put the Lord Jesus to death, and the prophets too. And now they have been persecuting us, and acting in a way that cannot please God and makes
16 them the enemies of the whole human race, ·because they are hindering us from preaching to the pagans and trying to save them. They never stop trying to finish off the sins they have begun, but retribution is overtaking them at last.

✠

The detailed presentation of the initial statement found in 1:2–10 now moves from Paul's role and experience (2:1–12) to that of the Thessalonians (2:13–16). Gospel proclamation is thus a process of communication in which the addressees are no less important than the proclaimer. Indeed the response of the former is the basis of Paul's thanksgiving. The Thessalonians had received Paul's word as the very word of God, and that word now abides within them, actively constituting them as believers (2:13). Consequently, the imitation of Paul and openness to the life which he gave to them was no human phenomenon. Through his preaching in word and deed, they were given the word and life of God, and it is as such that they received it. Together with Paul and his colleagues, the Thessalonians could consequently claim God as their Father (1:1,3–4).

With verse 14, Paul extends the principle of imitation away from his own immediate efforts to the churches of Judaea. Suffering is thus situated in the broader perspectives of early Christian history. In their imitation of Paul, the Thessalonians reflected the experience of the earliest churches, which had suffered from Jewish persecution, just as the Thessalonians themselves had recently suffered at the hands of their fellows.

Ultimately, however, the Thessalonian church was imitating the experience of the Lord Jesus, whom the Jews had put to death, as well as the prophets before him (2:15a). Consequently, Paul's own sufferings and those of the Thessalonians are but a link in a pattern of persecution which reaches back to the very origins of Christianity and even to the history of Israel which led to it. The references to Jesus as Lord evokes the resurrection (1:10) and points to the happy outcome of persecution which leads to a new life in God. In 2:15b–16, Paul points to the motivation behind the persecution, which from the beginning has sprung from resistance to the proclamation of the gospel beyond Judaism to all humankind.

STUDY QUESTIONS: How does the principle of imitation contribute to Paul's theology of history? What is significant about the title "Lord" in 1:10?

1 Thessalonians 2:17 – 3:5
TIMOTHY'S MISSION

17 A short time after we had been separated from you—in body but never in thought, brothers—we had an especially strong desire and longing to see 18 you face to face again, ·and we tried hard to come and visit you; I, Paul, tried more than once, but 19 Satan prevented us. ·What do you think is our pride and our joy? You are; and you will be the crown of which we shall be proudest in the pres- 20 ence of our Lord Jesus when he comes; ·you are our pride and our joy.

3 ¹ When we could not bear the waiting any longer, we decided it would be best to be left 2 without a companion at Athens, and ·sent our brother Timothy, who is God's helper in spread- ing the Good News of Christ, to keep you firm 3 and strong in the faith ·and prevent any of you from being unsettled by the present troubles. As you know, these are bound to come our way: 4 when we were with you, we warned you that we must expect to have persecutions to bear, and that is what has happened now, as you have found 5 out. ·That is why, when I could not stand waiting any longer, I sent to assure myself of your faith: I was afraid the Tempter might have tried you too hard, and all our work might have been wasted.

✠

Paul now addresses the immediate circumstances which have led to the writing of the letter

(2:17–3:11). First he describes his intention to visit the Thessalonians personally and indicates how he had eventually sent Timothy to them (2:17–3:5).

From 1:2–2:16, we sensed the strong bond which united Paul and the Thessalonians, a bond strengthened by a common share in persecution and suffering. This bond reverberated in Paul's human attitude and transcended face-to-face separation, but it did not diminish his desire to see them (2:17). Accordingly he had repeatedly tried to return to them, but to no avail, so great were the forces of evil, Satan, which stood in the way (2:18). The persecution which forced Paul's departure from Thessalonika had thus continued unabated, preventing his return to that city.

The reason for Paul's intense desire lay in his appreciation that those who had received God's living word from him were his hope, his joy and the crown in which he would find his pride at the coming of our Lord Jesus (2:19–20). Paul's pride thus lies not in himself, but in those whom God had engendered through his efforts.

Unwilling to further delay a visit, Paul had decided to remain alone with Silvanus at Athens and to send Timothy in his place. Timothy was Paul's brother not only in faith and fellowship but also in the Christian mission. Together with Paul and Silvanus, he was God's helper in spreading the Good News of Christ. Paul had commissioned him to strengthen the church of the Thessalonians at a time when persecution threatened its peace (3:1–3).

Paul then recalls how he had warned them to expect such persecutions, so that they should have no cause for consternation. We thus have an indication that the persecutions which had led to Paul's departure from Thessalonika continued to menace the community. The

apostle had sent Timothy to them out of concern that
the Tempter might have pressed the church beyond its
youthful strength (3:4–5).

STUDY QUESTIONS: What was Timothy's role in the
                ongoing evangelization of Thessa-
                lonika? Was letter writing Paul's
                preferred mode of communication?

1 Thessalonians 3:6–13
TIMOTHY'S RETURN

⁶ However, Timothy is now back from you and he has given us good news of your faith and your love, telling us that you always remember us with pleasure and want to see us quite as much as we ⁷ want to see you. ·And so, brothers, your faith has been a great comfort to us in the middle of our ⁸ own troubles and sorrows; ·now we can breathe again, as you are still holding firm in the Lord. ⁹ How can we thank God enough for you, for all the joy we feel before our God on your account? ¹⁰ We are earnestly praying night and day to be able to see you face to face again and make up any shortcomings in your faith.

¹¹ May God our Father himself, and our Lord Jesus Christ, make it easy for us to come to you. ¹² May the Lord be generous in increasing your love and make you love one another and the ¹³ whole human race as much as we love you. ·And may he so confirm your hearts in holiness that you may be blameless in the sight of our God and Father when our Lord Jesus Christ comes with all his saints.

✠

Continuing with the recent events which led to the writing of the present letter, Paul now tells of Timothy's return with good news (3:6–10). Faith and love are alive and well at Thessalonika, and the apostles have not been forgotten. Desire for a reunion between Paul and the Thessalonians is mutual. Comforted and joyful, Paul explicitly recalls the sentiments of thanksgiving (1:2, 2:13, 3:9) which underlie this entire first part of the letter (1:2 – 3:13). Thanksgiving for the past and the present issues into prayer for the future (3:10–13).

Paul's prayer is that he might once again see the Thessalonians face to face (3:10–11), a dominant theme in 2:17 – 3:13. Paul thus thought of the present letter as a means of communication when personal presence and the spoken word were impossible. The written word, however, could never replace a personal visit. As a temporary measure, it was meant to prepare for such a visit. The purpose of Paul's coming would be to remedy any shortcomings in faith (3:10).

Paul's prayer is that the Thessalonians grow in love among themselves and for the entire human race (3:12, 2:15b–16) and that they be confirmed in holiness for the day of Christ's return (3:13). In reverse order, these three elements, namely holiness, love and faith, outline the exhortation which now follows (4:1 – 5:11).

Thanksgiving for faith and love in the past and present are the ground of prayerful hope for the future (1:2–3, 3:6–13). Without faith and love, there is no hope. Without thanksgiving, there is no prayer.

STUDY QUESTIONS: Through what steps does Paul's message lead to prayer? What are the basic elements of Paul's prayer, and how are they related to the exhortation (4:1 – 5:11)?

1 Thessalonians 4:1–12
A PLEA FOR HOLINESS AND LOVE

¹ 4 Finally, brothers, we urge you and appeal to you in the Lord Jesus to make more and more progress in the kind of life that you are meant to live: the life that God wants, as you learned from ² us, and as you are already living it. ·You have not forgotten the instructions we gave you on the authority of the Lord Jesus.

³ What God wants is for you all to be holy. He ⁴ wants you to keep away from fornication, ·and each one of you to know how to use the body that belongs to him in a way that is holy and hon- ⁵ orable, ·not giving way to selfish lust like the pa- ⁶ gans who do not know God. ·He wants nobody at all ever to sin by taking advantage of a brother in these matters; the Lord always punishes sins of that sort, as we told you before and assured you. ⁷ We have been called by God to be holy, not to be ⁸ immoral; ·in other words, anyone who objects is not objecting to a human authority, but to God, who gives you his Holy Spirit.

⁹ As for loving our brothers, there is no need for anyone to write to you about that, since you have learned from God yourselves to love one another, ¹⁰ and in fact this is what you are doing with all the brothers throughout the whole of Macedonia. However, we do urge you, brothers, to go on ¹¹ making even greater progress ·and to make a point of living quietly, attending to your own business and earning your living, just as we told ¹² you to, ·so that you are seen to be respectable by those outside the Church, though you do not have to depend on them.

☩

A brief introduction (4:1–2) marks the transition to the second part of Paul's letter. The writer's stance is now one of urgent appeal for continued progress in the life which God wants, a life the addressees had learned from Paul and which they were actually living. Paul's historical and experiential point of reference is thus his earlier preaching while at Thessalonika as well as the way of life which was already interiorized by the church.

Paul's earlier instruction had been given on the authority of the Lord Jesus (4:2) and his present appeal is grounded in the same authoritative source (4:1). Indeed, Paul's word had been accepted as the word of God (2:13). We are thus provided with the grounds for viewing the written word as a Christian word of God. The following verses provide a unique insight into aspects of life which sprang immediately from the Gospel's initial proclamation.

After the introduction, Paul recalls his teaching on holiness (4:3–8), the theme on which his prayer had concluded (3:13). In so doing, he articulates what God wants (4:3, 4:1), namely that those who have been called to holiness refrain from all that is unholy (4:7). For men and women whose life had unfolded in the pagan context of Thessalonika, there were special demands in the area of sexual morality. Those who do not know God may well give themselves to selfish lust, but such behavior can have no place in the lives of those who have come to know God. Some seem to have been objecting to Paul's teaching in these matters.

Paul responds that their objection is actually directed to God who gives the Spirit of holiness (4:8).

The exhortation then turns to love of the brothers, that is, to the love which should characterize the life of the community (4:9–12, 3:12). Paul had already expressed his gratitude that the Thessalonians were steeped in that love (1:3) and he had just been reassured of their fidelity in love by Timothy (3:6). There were consequently no reasons to write to them concerning this matter. Their love, like the example of their faith (1:7–8), already had spread through Macedonia (4:10a). However, Paul still found it necessary to urge them forward in a few matters on which he had already spoken to them. In particular, each one was to work at earning a living and not to rely on the charitable support of the community (4:10b–11). This is important for their apostolic witness (4:12).

STUDY QUESTIONS: What grounds does Paul provide for viewing his letter as the word of God? What is the relationship between love or charity and working for one's livelihood?

1 Thessalonians 4:13 – 5:11
IMPORTANT MATTERS OF FAITH

13   We want you to be quite certain, brothers, about those who have died, to make sure that you do not grieve about them, like the other people
14 who have no hope. ·We believe that Jesus died and rose again, and that it will be the same for those who have died in Jesus: God will bring them with
15 him. ·We can tell you this from the Lord's own teaching, that any of us who are left alive until the Lord's coming will not have any advantage over
16 those who have died. ·At the trumpet of God, the voice of the archangel will call out the command and the Lord himself will come down from heaven; those who have died in Christ will be the
17 first to rise, ·and then those of us who are still alive will be taken up in the clouds, together with them, to meet the Lord in the air. So we shall stay
18 with the Lord for ever. ·With such thoughts as these you should comfort one another.

5   1 You will not be expecting us to write anything to you, brothers, about "times and seasons,"
2 since you know very well that the Day of the Lord is going to come like a thief in the night.
3 It is when people are saying, "How quiet and peaceful it is" that the worst suddenly happens, as suddenly as labor pains come on a pregnant woman; and there will be no way for anybody to evade it.
4   But it is not as if you live in the dark, my brothers, for that Day to overtake you like a thief.
5 No, you are all sons of light and sons of the day:
6 we do not belong to the night or to darkness, ·so we should not go on sleeping, as everyone else
7 does, but stay wide awake and sober. ·Night is the

time for sleepers to sleep and drunkards to be
8 drunk, ·but we belong to the day and we should
be sober; let us put on faith and love for a breast-
plate, and the hope of salvation for a helmet.
9 God never meant us to experience the Retribution, but to win salvation through our Lord Jesus
10 Christ, ·who died for us so that, alive or dead, we
11 should still live united to him. ·So give encouragement to each other, and keep strengthening one
another, as you do already.

✠

Three times in the letter's long thanksgiving section
Paul had referred to the final coming of God's Son,
our Lord Jesus Christ (1:10, 2:20, 3:13). Two major
problems in the church's faith regarding that coming
are now addressed at some length. Paul thus takes up
the first of the three elements outlined in 3:10–13.

The first problem concerns the unexpected death of
members of the community (4:13–18). Apparently,
the Thessalonians had not anticipated that any of them
would die before the Lord's coming, and this had
shaken their faith in the entire Gospel's message. In response, Paul develops aspects of the Gospel on which
he may not have dwelt during his visit, and he enables
the Thessalonians to integrate Christian death in their
grasp of the Gospel.

Like the struggles and persecutions of the present
time (2:14–15), the death of Christians is closely related to that of Jesus. Jesus' death had led to the resurrection; so would it be with those who had died in him
(4:14). To die in Jesus is to die while associated with
him in a life which risks even death in the service of
the Gospel (2:8). Appealing to the Lord's own teaching, Paul then describes a scenario aimed at showing

how those who will still be living at the Lord's coming will have no advantage over the dead (4:15–17). Such is the basis of Christian hope (4:13) and mutual comfort (4:18). In his description of a moment which transcends history and earthly realities, Paul appeals to the symbols of Jewish apocalyptic and interprets these in terms of Christ. He thus finds appropriate language to present the humanly indescribable.

The second problem concerns the precise time of Christ's coming (5:1–11). The church must not think that their persecution is chronologically related to the end of time and the return of Christ. All such speculation is groundless and idle. The Thessalonians should already know that the return of Christ will occur when least expected (5:1–3). This does not mean that they are in the dark. On the contrary, as Christians they walk in the light of faith, love and hope, and Paul exhorts them to remain in that light (5:4–8). God intends that they win salvation, not retribution (5:9, 1:10) which is reserved for their persecutors (2:16). Returning to the theme of 4:13–18, Paul ends this section by calling for mutual encouragement and strengthening (5:10–11) as he had called for mutual comfort (4:18).

STUDY QUESTIONS: What two problems did the community encounter with regard to Christ's second coming? Do Paul's responses to these problems retain any relevance for today?

1 Thessalonians 5:12–28
FINAL APPEAL, BLESSING AND FAREWELL

¹² We appeal to you, my brothers, to be considerate to those who are working among you and ¹³ are above you in the Lord as your teachers. ·Have the greatest respect and affection for them because of their work.

¹⁴ Be at peace among yourselves. ·And this is what we ask you to do, brothers: warn the idlers, give courage to those who are apprehensive, care for ¹⁵ the weak and be patient with everyone. ·Make sure that people do not try to take revenge; you must all think of what is best for each other and ¹⁶ for the community. ·Be happy at all times; ·pray ¹⁷ ¹⁸ constantly; ·and for all things give thanks to God, because this is what God expects you to do in Christ Jesus.

¹⁹ ²⁰ Never try to suppress the Spirit ·or treat the gift ²¹ of prophecy with contempt; ·think before you do ²² anything—hold on to what is good ·and avoid every form of evil.

²³ May the God of peace make you perfect and holy; and may you all be kept safe and blameless, spirit, soul and body, for the coming of our Lord ²⁴ Jesus Christ. ·God has called you and he will not fail you.

²⁵ Pray for us, my brothers.

²⁶ ²⁷ Greet all the brothers with the holy kiss. ·My orders, in the Lord's name, are that this letter is to be read to all the brothers.

²⁸ The grace of our Lord Jesus Christ be with you.

✠

We now come to a series of closing exhortations, bearing on respect for Christian teachers (5:12–13), peace and appropriate attitudes and behavior among members of the community (5:14–18), and openness to the Spirit and the gift of prophecy (5:19–22).

It thus becomes clear that Christian teachers had emerged in the community in the wake of Paul's apostolic visit. It was important that such teachers be recognized and accepted (5:12–13).

The peace of the community was troubled on several counts. Not all worked with equal dedication. Hence Paul's earlier indication that he himself, whom they were called to emulate, had worked hard so as not to place a burden on the community's charity (2:9). There were also those who were apprehensive or weak, and this called for patience and discerning attention. Constant prayer and thanksgiving would be the guarantors of peace (5:14–18).

Finally, there appears to have been discord over the manifestations of God's Spirit and resistance to the gift of prophecy in their midst (5:19–22). Prophecy, it should be recalled, is the human utterance of God's word, and Paul himself had been a prophet among them (2:13). The problems which the church of Thessalonika began to experience would one day loom extremely large at Corinth from which Paul was now writing (1 Co 12–14).

The first letter to the church at Thessalonika concludes with a prayer of blessing, an appeal for prayer, a request that the letter be read to all in the assembly, where the Christians manifested their love for one another, and a prayerful wish that the grace of Christ be with them (5:23–28). The conclusion thus reiterates and develops the opening greeting (1:1) that the church at Thessalonika receive grace (5:28) and mir-

ror the God of peace in its holiness in view of the return of Christ (5:23). As in the body of the letter
(1:10, 2:20, 3:13, 4:13–18, 5:1–11), the return of
Christ continues to define the horizon of Christian life
and effort.

STUDY QUESTIONS: What is prophecy? How are the letter's concluding statements related
to the introductory greeting and the
body of the letter?

2 Thessalonians
The Second Letter of Paul
to the Church in Thessalonika

INTRODUCTION

Paul's first letter to the Christians of Thessalonika, exuberant and hopeful as it addressed the problems which had emerged in that community, did not resolve all the issues troubling the young church. It may be that, in his relief and joy over the news concerning the success of the mission, Paul had not appreciated the full scope or depth of the community's problems. Accordingly, but a few months after writing the first letter and after receiving further news from Thessalonika, Paul dictated a second letter, whose conclusion bears the authoritative stamp of his own signature (3:17–18). This letter, the second to the church of Thessalonika, was also written from Corinth.

As in the first letter, Paul repeatedly recalls the teaching he had shared during his short apostolic stay in the city. On key issues, however, such as the coming of the Lord (2:1–12), idleness and disunity (3:6–15), he expresses himself more insistently or at greater length than in the previous letter. Further, we note that temporal distance, fresh preoccupations at Corinth, and the aggravation of the situation at Thessalonika itself have weakened the tone of intimate warmth which pervaded the previous letter. In the second letter to the church at Thessalonika, Paul appears less immediately involved and more distant than in the first.

In reading the second letter, which is even shorter than the first, we are invited to join a community in which the initial joy and unity of the Gospel of salvation finds itself increasingly threatened by the harsh

realities of life. We are thus called to join the church of
Thessalonika in the challenges of Christian maturation.
We are also invited to join Paul in the assumption of
ongoing responsibility for those with whom we have
shared and lived the gospel, however difficult this may
be, and however pressing the demands of life elsewhere.

Like the first letter, the second includes an address
(1:1–2), a long section on thanksgiving (1:3–3:5),
an exhortation (3:6–15) and concluding blessings
(3:16–18). As in the first, the tone of exhortation pervades the entire letter, a fact which led to the inclusion
of considerations on the final coming in the first part of
the letter (1:3–3:5) rather than in the exhortation
proper (3:6–15). The structure of the letter is thus
governed by the author's apostolic and pastoral intent,
in which doctrinal and ethical considerations work together for a common purpose.

2 Thessalonians 1:1–12
GREETING AND THANKSGIVING

¹ From Paul, Silvanus and Timothy, to the Church in Thessalonika which is in God our ² Father and the Lord Jesus Christ; ·wishing you grace and peace from God the Father and the Lord Jesus Christ.

³ We feel we must be continually thanking God for you, brothers; quite rightly, because your faith is growing so wonderfully and the love that you ⁴ have for one another never stops increasing; ·and among the churches of God we can take special pride in you for your constancy and faith under all the persecutions and troubles you have to bear. ⁵ It all shows that God's judgment is just, and the purpose of it is that you may be found worthy of the kingdom of God; it is for the sake of this that you are suffering now.

⁶ God will very rightly repay with injury those ⁷ who are injuring you, ·and reward you, who are suffering now, with the same peace as he will give us, when the Lord Jesus appears from heaven with ⁸ the angels of his power. ·He will come in flaming fire to impose the penalty on all who do not acknowledge God and refuse to accept the Good ⁹ News of our Lord Jesus. ·It will be their punishment to be lost eternally, excluded from the presence of the Lord and from the glory of his ¹⁰ strength ·on that day when he comes to be glorified among his saints and seen in his glory by all who believe in him; and you are believers, through our witness.

¹¹ Knowing this, we pray continually that our God will make you worthy of his call, and by his power fulfill all your desires for goodness and

complete all that you have been doing through
12 faith; ·because in this way the name of our Lord
Jesus Christ will be glorified in you and you in
him, by the grace of our God and the Lord Jesus
Christ.

✠

The letter begins with an address which is identical
to that of 1 Th 1:1, save that the grace and peace are
explicitly said to be from God the Father and the Lord
Jesus Christ (1:1–2). Silvanus and Timothy are still
with Paul at Corinth, and they are again named as co-
senders of the letter.

The persistence of difficulties at Thessalonika has
not muted Paul's attitude of thanksgiving. The latter
constitutes the dominant theme of the first part of the
letter (1:3–3:5) and is explicitly noted in 1:3–12 and
2:13–3:5. As in 1 Thessalonians, this first major unit
climaxes in a statement on prayer and of prayer
(3:1–5).

The reason for thanksgiving lies in the Thessalonians' faith and love, which have never ceased growing,
even under the pressure of persecution and troubles
(1:3–4). A theological basis is adduced for these: persecutions are grounded in God's just judgment. Their
purpose, and that of the suffering they cause, is to
make the Christians worthy of the kingdom of God
(1:5; see 1 Th 2:12). The Christians come to glory
through suffering.

In 1 Th 2:16, retribution for the persecutors was
only briefly mentioned. However, to bolster the Thessalonians in their fidelity, Paul now treats of this matter
at greater length (1:6–10). God will reward believers
with peace but the persecutors will be repaid with

eternal punishment and excluded from the Lord's presence on the day of his coming in glory. To enrich this statement concerning the persecutors, Paul draws on a series of biblical expressions from Jr 10:25, and Is 2:10–17, 49:3, 66:5, 66:15. The very need for such language and the length of the presentation indicates Paul's awareness of the gravity of a situation which is nevertheless not hopeless.

Paul then moves from thanksgiving to prayer of petition. This movement, like that from faith to love and hope, is a normal one. In this instance, however, it is also reinforced by urgent need and the danger of faltering. The Christians have been called, but they will be shown worthy of their call only when its purpose is finally fulfilled with the glorification of Christ in them and their own glorification in him (1:11–12). The glory of Christ on the day of his coming is thus intimately bound up with the unfailing constancy of those he has called.

STUDY QUESTIONS: What are the grounds for Paul's thanksgiving? Why does Paul provide a fairly extensive treatment of retribution in this letter?

2 Thessalonians 2:1–12
THE COMING OF CHRIST

¹ 2 To turn now, brothers, to the coming of our
Lord Jesus Christ and how we shall all be
² gathered around him: ·please do not get excited
too soon or alarmed by any prediction or rumor
or any letter claiming to come from us, implying
that the Day of the Lord has already arrived.
³ Never let anyone deceive you in this way.

It cannot happen until the Great Revolt has
taken place and the Rebel, the Lost One, has
⁴ appeared. ·This is the Enemy, the one who claims
to be so much greater than all that men call
"god," so much greater than anything that is wor-
shiped, that he enthrones himself in God's sanc-
⁵ tuary and claims that he is God. ·Surely you remember me telling you about this when I was
⁶ with you? ·And you know, too, what is still holding him back from appearing before his ap-
⁷ pointed time. ·Rebellion is at its work already, but
in secret, and the one who is holding it back has
⁸ first to be removed ·before the Rebel appears
openly. The Lord will kill him with the breath of
his mouth and will annihilate him with his glorious appearance at his coming.

⁹ But when the Rebel comes, Satan will set to
work: there will be all kinds of miracles and a
¹⁰ deceptive show of signs and portents, ·and everything evil that can deceive those who are bound
for destruction because they would not grasp the
love of the truth which could have saved them.
¹¹ The reason why God is sending a power to delude
¹² them and make them believe what is untrue ·is to
condemn all who refused to believe in the truth
and chose wickedness instead.

✠

The question of the Lord's coming (2:1-12) is
taken up in this first part of the letter and framed by
the two passages explicitly devoted to thanksgiving
(1:3-12, 2:13-3:5). In 1 Thessalonians, the same
question (4:13-18 and especially 5:1-11) constituted
part of the exhortation (4:1-5:22). It has thus become a major concern, seriously affecting the grounds
of Paul's thanksgiving.

Paul had already written to the Thessalonians that
they should not be concerned about the precise time of
the Lord's coming. This would only distract them from
constant preparedness (1 Th 5:1-11). It appears,
however, that the strength of the opposition encountered was leading some to conclude that the Day of the
Lord had already arrived, and the air was filled with
predictions and rumors. Paul dismisses all of these as
deception. Ever the master of rhetoric, he adds that
even a letter from him and his fellow missionaries
would have to be ignored if it supported such rumors
(2:1-3a).

To substantiate his position, Paul recalls what he
had already taught while at Thessalonika (2:4b). The
need to respond to the current nervous agitation super-
sedes his pastoral preoccupation with wakefulness and
readiness (1 Th 5:1-11) and he outlines the events
which will precede the end when Christ does actually
come (2:3b-12). His presentation of these events is
meant to relativize the community's present troubles,
which are minimal in comparison with what is yet to
come.

Before the Lord comes, all the forces of evil will be

unleashed in a Great Revolt, when one called the
Rebel, the Lost One and the Enemy will try to usurp
God's position in the Kingdom (2:3b–4). At that time,
Satan will be at work with miracles, signs and portents,
deceiving those who have rejected the truth unto their
own condemnation (2:9–12). This state of rebellion is
already at work, but only in secret, and the time of its
full manifestation has not yet come. When the Rebel
does appear, the Lord will also come and destroy him
by his glorious appearance (2:5–8).

Paul thus presents the history of Christianity and of
the Gospel mission in terms of their climactic fulfillment
and as a decisive confrontation between good and evil.
All must know what is ultimately at stake as the community responds to difficulties from within and persecution from without.

STUDY QUESTIONS: What is the difference between the
structure of 2 Thessalonians and of
1 Thessalonians? Why does Paul
discuss the Lord's second coming
in detail?

2 Thessalonians 2:13 – 3:5
THANKSGIVING AND PRAYER

¹³ But we feel that we must be continually thanking God for you, brothers whom the Lord loves, because God chose you from the beginning to be saved by the sanctifying Spirit and by faith in the ¹⁴ truth. ·Through the Good News that we brought he called you to this so that you should share the ¹⁵ glory of our Lord Jesus Christ. ·Stand firm, then, brothers, and keep the traditions that we taught you, whether by word of mouth or by letter. ¹⁶ May our Lord Jesus Christ himself, and God our Father who has given us his love and, through his grace, such inexhaustible comfort and such sure ¹⁷ hope, ·comfort you and strengthen you in everything good that you do or say.

¹ 3 Finally, brothers, pray for us; pray that the Lord's message may spread quickly and be re-² ceived with honor as it was among you; ·and pray that we may be preserved from the interference of bigoted and evil people, for faith is not given ³ to everyone. ·But the Lord is faithful, and he will give you strength and guard you from the ⁴ evil one, ·and we, in the Lord, have every confidence that you are doing and will go on doing ⁵ all that we tell you. ·May the Lord turn your hearts toward the love of God and the fortitude of Christ.

✠

Given the community's present problems, thanksgiving for God's election of the Thessalonians for salvation (2:13–14) is consequently supplemented by an

appeal to stand firm (2:15). God's choice of them
through Paul's bringing of the good news had a purpose which has yet to be fulfilled. Fidelity to the traditions which Paul had taught by word of mouth and in 1
Thessalonians would ensure their eventual sharing in
the glory of our Lord Jesus Christ.

Paul then turns to prayer (2:16–17) as he did in 1
Th 3:11–13. His prayer is that the Lord Jesus Christ
and God our Father strengthen the Christians that the
love which they had received might one day blossom in
the fulfillment of their hope. Echoing the greeting of
1:2, Paul thus wants to guarantee fidelity along the
historical path which leads from the community's origins to its ultimate destiny.

In praying for others, Paul and his two colleagues
also ask for prayers on their behalf. More specifically
they ask that the Thessalonians pray for the success of
their mission, that their word, which is the word of
God (1 Th 2:13) and the Lord's word, be received
elsewhere as it had been received among them (3:1).
Like the Thessalonians, Paul also finds his efforts ob-
structed by bigoted and faithless people, and he asks
for prayers that he be preserved from their interference
(3:2).

Concluding the letter's first long unit, Paul affirms
his trust that the Lord, in his faithfulness, will answer
his prayer positively, and that the strength he gives will
be reflected in the faithfulness of the Thessalonians
(3:3–4). The love of God and the fortitude of Christ
sum up his prayer for the struggling church (3:5).

STUDY QUESTIONS: What are the elements of Paul's
prayer in 2 Th 2:16–17? How do
these compare with those of 1 Th
3:11–13?

EXHORTATION AND FAREWELL

⁶   In the name of the Lord Jesus Christ, we urge you, brothers, to keep away from any of the brothers who refuses to work or to live according to the tradition we passed on to you.

⁷   You know how you are supposed to imitate us: now we were not idle when we were with you, ⁸ nor did we ever have our meals at anyone's table without paying for them; no, we worked night and day, slaving and straining, so as not to be a ⁹ burden on any of you. ·This was not because we had no right to be, but in order to make ourselves an example for you to follow.

¹⁰   We gave you a rule when we were with you: not to let anyone have any food if he refused to ¹¹ do any work. ·Now we hear that there are some of you who are living in idleness, doing no work themselves but interfering with everyone else's. ¹² In the Lord Jesus Christ, we order and call on people of this kind to go on quietly working and earning the food that they eat.

¹³   My brothers, never grow tired of doing what ¹⁴ is right. ·If anyone refuses to obey what I have written in this letter, take note of him and have nothing to do with him, so that he will feel that ¹⁵ he is in the wrong; ·though you are not to regard him as an enemy but as a brother in need of correction.

¹⁶   May the Lord of peace himself give you peace all the time and in every way. The Lord be with you all.

¹⁷   From me, PAUL, these greetings in my own handwriting, which is the mark of genuineness in

[18] every letter; this is my own writing. ·May the grace of our Lord Jesus Christ be with you all.

✠

As in 1 Thessalonians, the theme of thanksgiving is now followed by an exhortation (3:6–15). Indeed exhortation had constituted an important substratum of 1:3–3:5. However, with 3:6, it becomes the explicit and dominant element in Paul's pastoral message.

Paul urges the community to disassociate itself from any who refuse to work (3:6a). This had been introduced as a relatively minor problem in 1 Th 5:14. No longer. Paul warns the community not to become allies of idlers. Rather they are to live according to the tradition passed on to them (3:6b). Idleness is the main point of 3:6–15. The appeal to tradition echoes 2:15.

The tradition had been communicated by Paul's way of life (1 Th 1:5) as well as by word of mouth and letter (2 Th 2:15). Fundamentally, it called for the imitation of Paul who was not idle while at Thessalonika (3:7). The same theme of apostolic imitation had been introduced in more general terms in 1 Th 1:5–6. Paul had not accepted meals at anyone's table without paying for them in some way, and this had required unceasing hard work on his part. The right to hospitality and the duty to extend it must consequently be balanced by one's sense of responsibility to assume the burden of the community. All share in the same rights and duties. In all this, Paul had been an example to be followed (3:8–9).

As on several other occasions in the two letters to the Thessalonians (1 Th 1:5–6, 2:1–12,13, 3:4, 4:1,11; 2 Th 2:5,14–15), Paul recalls his teaching during his period of evangelization at Thessalonika. At that time, he had issued a general rule: those who refuse to work should not be given anything to eat (3:10). Some are not following that rule, and in their idleness they even interfere with the work of others (3:11). Appealing for a faithful return to tradition (3:12), Paul asks that his admonition be accepted and that the wayward be duly corrected (3:15).

The letter concludes with liturgically inspired greetings (3:16,17) comparable to those of 1 Th 5:23,28. These were most appropriate since Paul's message was to be read in the community's assembly. The apostle's authoritative word is bolstered by his own signature (3:17). Paul clearly intends that his letter be taken seriously.

STUDY QUESTIONS: How does Paul's principle of imitation operate in 3:6–18? Why did Paul use liturgical language in his concluding greetings?

1 Corinthians
The First Letter of Paul
to the Church at Corinth

INTRODUCTION

Having written two letters from Corinth (1 and 2 Thessalonians), Paul once again takes to the written word in the service of the Gospel. This time, however, his letter is written to Corinth, a church in which Paul had spent many months of careful and fundamental evangelization. After his departure, the community came upon many internal difficulties, most of which stemmed from a tendency to individualistic self-expression and lack of effective and recognized leadership. He now writes (ca. 56) to the Corinthians from Ephesus (1 Co 16:8), the capital of the Roman province of Asia, where he is devoting an extended period to evangelical work.

After the address and greeting (1:1–3), Paul includes a thanksgiving unit (1:4–9) and proceeds to the first part of the letter where he takes up matters brought to his attention by members of Chloe's household (1:10 – 4:21) or which were general knowledge (5:1 – 6:20). The second part of the letter addresses questions and points included in a letter which Stephanas, Fortunatus and Achaicus (16:17) had brought from Corinth (7:1 – 16:4).

These two sections of the letter reveal a community struggling with developmental problems which we would expect of a young community whose beliefs and way of life differed sharply from the bustling urban environment in which it had been planted. In a sense, 1 Corinthians provides a case study for grasping the challenges of any community which must cope with the industrial and commercial life of a major port city where permanent inhabitants are buffeted by the strong influence of many transients, whose roots in the city are minimal or nil.

It is from this point of view that we are invited to read 1 Corinthians and to follow Paul as he makes his way through the manifold difficulties. We have much to learn from the way he establishes priorities and takes pastoral positions which may not be absolute and for-ever valid but which are clearly called for by the situa-tion at hand.

The letter's conclusion (16:5–24) evokes some of the personalism which was so pronounced in 1 Thes-salonians. Once again we find ourselves in a world of people on mission, of men and women who mean something to one another and complement one an-other's efforts. With its recall of names familiar from 1:10 – 4:21, the conclusion provides the letter with a strong sense of unity. The liturgically inspired phrases with which it ends (16:19–24) evoke the assembly in which the letter would be read at Corinth. That assem-bly continues to be the privileged context for reading the letter today.

1 Corinthians 1:1–9
ADDRESS AND THANKSGIVING

¹ I, Paul, appointed by God to be an apostle, together with brother Sosthenes, send greetings ² to the church of God in Corinth, to the holy people of Jesus Christ, who are called to take their place among all the saints everywhere who pray to our Lord Jesus Christ; for he is their Lord no less ³ than ours. ·May God our Father and the Lord Jesus Christ send you grace and peace.

⁴ I never stop thanking God for all the graces ⁵ you have received through Jesus Christ. ·I thank him that you have been enriched in so many ways, especially in your teachers and preachers; ⁶ the witness to Christ has indeed been strong ⁷ among you ·so that you will not be without any of the gifts of the Spirit while you are waiting for ⁸ our Lord Jesus Christ to be revealed; ·and he will keep you steady and without blame until the last ⁹ day, the day of our Lord Jesus Christ, ·because God by calling you has joined you to his Son, Jesus Christ; and God is faithful.

✠

Paul's first letter to the church at Corinth opens with a formal address (1:1–3) and a sharply defined expression of thanksgiving (1:4–9). Sosthenes joins Paul as a co-sender, but from the letter's predominant use of the first person singular we must conclude that his role was less significant than that of Silvanus and Timothy in the Thessalonian letters. Both the address and the

thanksgiving unit prepare the readers for the body of
the letter by carefully positioning Paul and the Corinthian church within a common Christian enterprise.

Paul is an apostle, appointed by God, and it is as
such that he had evangelized Corinth and that he now
writes to its Christians (1:1). The church which re-
sulted from Paul's efforts is the church of God, the
same who had accredited Paul for his mission. Even as
he greets the Corinthians, Paul reminds them of their
calling. His description of the church is at once a
teaching, an admonition and an exhortation, betraying
Paul's attitude and indirectly setting forth the letter's
underlying purpose. Have the Corinthians forgotten
that Jesus Christ is their Lord no less than that of Paul
and Sosthenes? Paul thus hints at the disunity and the
factionalism which has now come to plague the
Corinthian church (1:2). Against this background the
prayerful wish for grace and peace appears far from
casual (1:3).

The theme of thanksgiving, which characterized the
first major unit of both 1 and 2 Thessalonians, has now
developed into a formal unit. Summarizing the constant
prayer of gratitude which he addresses to God, Paul
reminds the Corinthians of the grace they have received
(1:4) and especially of their enrichment through
teachers and preachers (1:5). The work of Apollos,
who had followed Paul to Corinth, and of those cur-
rently active in the community is thus viewed positively, in spite of the many difficulties which the
Corinthians are experiencing. In the letter Paul will
take great pains to situate Apollos' teaching in relation
to his own and their ministries will be related to the
many gifts or charisms which characterize the community.

The Corinthians must recognize, however, that such

gifts are not God's definitive manifestation (cf. 4:8)
but relative to the full revelation of Jesus Christ
(1:6–7). God is faithful, and he will keep the church,
which he has called and joined to his Son, steady and
without blame until the day of Christ's coming
(1:8–9). Of this Paul is confident and the community
must share the same confidence as it responds to its
present internal conflicts and difficulties.

STUDY QUESTION: How does Paul's thanksgiving announce some of the main themes
and concerns of the letter?

1 Corinthians 1:10 – 6:20
TROUBLING REPORTS FROM CORINTH

In the first part of the letter (1:10 – 6:20), Paul deals with four important matters which had been brought to his attention by members of Chloe's household (1:11) and by general reports from Corinth (5:1). These matters are treated in four units, of which the first is by far the longest. The order in which they are presented is not determined by internal logic so much as by thematic association. As such, the theme with which each unit concludes suggests the subject to be treated in the next. The four units thus represent four links in a continuous chain of development.

First, there was the emergence of divisive factions in the Corinthian community (1:10 – 4:21). These factions invoke the names of Paul, Apollos, Cephas and even Christ as their rallying slogans (1:12). Paul responds by showing the radical inconsistency between such factionalism and the most basic expression and implications of the Gospel (1:10 – 2:5). After situating his own teaching in relation to a wisdom for which the Corinthians had obviously been unprepared (2:6 – 3:4), he develops the complementary relationship between Apollos and himself in the evangelization and catechesis of the community (3:5–17). Summarizing, he then concludes his position and gives special consideration to the matter of judging and being judged (3:18 – 4:21). In all of this, Paul focuses on the history of the community to provide an example which should enable the community to sort out the issues confronting it and resolve current problems (4:6).

Second, there was the community's failure to deal with a case of incest in its own membership (5:1–13). Paul's warnings against premature judgment (4:3–5) and his reflections on the basis of divine judgment (4:18–21) lead him to take up a situation where judgment is clearly required (5:12–13). He thus avoids the danger of misinterpretation and confusion which his absolute statements had occasioned on previous occasions (5:6–11, 6:12).

Third, the same theme of judgment called for a strong statement on the question of resolving internal community conflicts before non-Christian judges (6:1–8).

Fourth, the previous unit's concluding reflections on the way Christians are wronging one another (6:8) lead Paul to take up general matters of morality and the particular question of having sexual relations with a prostitute (6:9–20). As earlier concerning the factions (1:12), he must once again deal with the community's penchant for slogans (6:12–13).

1 Corinthians 1:10 – 2:5
FACTIONS: A CHRISTIAN CONTRADICTION

10 All the same, I do appeal to you, brothers, for the sake of our Lord Jesus Christ, to make up the differences between you, and instead of disagreeing among yourselves, to be united again in your
11 belief and practice. ·From what Chloe's people have been telling me, my dear brothers, it is clear that there are serious differences among you.
12 What I mean are all these slogans that you have, like: "I am for Paul," "I am for Apollos," "I am
13 for Cephas," "I am for Christ." ·Has Christ been parceled out? Was it Paul that was crucified for
14 you? Were you baptized in the name of Paul? ·I am thankful that I never baptized any of you after
15 Crispus and Gaius ·so none of you can say he
16 was baptized in my name. ·Then there was the family of Stephanas, of course, that I baptized too, but no one else as far as I can remember.
17 For Christ did not send me to baptize, but to preach the Good News, and not to preach that in the terms of philosophy in which the crucifixion
18 of Christ cannot be expressed. ·The language of the cross may be illogical to those who are not on the way to salvation, but those of us who are on
19 the way see it as God's power to save. ·As scripture says: I shall destroy the wisdom of the wise and bring to nothing all the learning of the
20 learned. ·Where are the philosophers now? Where are the scribes? Where are any of our thinkers today? Do you see now how God has shown up
21 the foolishness of human wisdom? ·If it was God's wisdom that human wisdom should not know God, it was because God wanted to save those who have faith through the foolishness of

22 the message that we preach. ·And so, while the Jews demand miracles and the Greeks look for
23 wisdom, ·here are we preaching a crucified Christ; to the Jews an obstacle that they cannot get over,
24 to the pagans madness, ·but to those who have been called, whether they are Jews or Greeks, a Christ who is the power and the wisdom of God.
25 For God's foolishness is wiser than human wisdom, and God's weakness is stronger than human strength.
26 Take yourselves for instance, brothers, at the time when you were called: how many of you were wise in the ordinary sense of the word, how many were influential people, or came from noble
27 families? ·No, it was to shame the wise that God chose what is foolish by human reckoning, and to shame what is strong that he chose what is weak
28 by human reckoning; ·those whom the world thinks common and contemptible are the ones that God has chosen—those who are nothing at
29 all to show up those who are everything. ·The human race has nothing to boast about to God,
30 but God has made you members of Christ Jesus and by God's doing he has become our wisdom, and our virtue, and our holiness, and our free-
31 dom. ·As scripture says: if anyone wants to boast, let him boast about the Lord.

2 As for me, brothers, when I came to you, it was not with any show of oratory or philosophy, but simply to tell you what God has guaran-
2 teed. ·During my stay with you, the only knowledge I claimed to have was about Jesus, and only
3 about him as the crucified Christ. ·Far from relying on any power of my own, I came among
4 you in great "fear and trembling" ·and in my speeches and the sermons that I gave, there were none of the arguments that belong to philosophy; only a demonstration of the power of the Spirit.
5 And I did this so that your faith should not depend on human philosophy but on the power of God.

✠

The body of the letter begins by treating a major problem of which Paul has been informed by members of Chloe's household (1:10–11). While at Ephesus, Paul thus keeps up-to-date on developments across the Aegean at Corinth. As later parts of the letter will make plain, the lines of communication between the communities at the two port cities were regular and multiple. In 1:10 – 4:21, which is structured like a complete letter but without concluding wishes, Paul responds to information brought by Christians whose business extends to both cities.

In 1:10–16, Paul describes the factions of which he has learned (1:10–12) and responds to the situation from two closely related points of view. First, such factions are incompatible with the community's relationship to Christ (1:13a). It makes no more sense to divide the community than it would to parcel out the one person of Christ. Second, the community is not founded on Paul but on Christ who was crucified for them. Their relationship to the one who baptized them must not obscure their common relationship to Christ. Paul is grateful that he had baptized very few. In the circumstances, the opposite would only have magnified the situation and occasioned greater disunity (1:13b–16).

Paul then outlines the essential element of the Christian mission, which is to preach the crucifixion of Christ in the face of all purely human expectations, whether Jewish or Gentile (1:17–25). The Corinthians have become infatuated by philosophical elaborations, which they see as replacing Paul's simple and unyielding message. The cross is divine wisdom, and it has revealed the foolishness of human wisdom. Such is the basic Christian paradox, and Paul refuses to be deflected from it. The crucified Christ is thus the foundation of all Christian reflection, and all else loses its meaning when the cross is shunted to the side or when the sharpness of its message is dulled by other considerations. This position retains all its relevance at a time when it has once again become necessary to affirm the evangelical basis of Christianity.

The letter then shows how the paradoxical association of divine strength and human weakness (1:25) is reflected in the Corinthian community (1:26–31) and in Paul's own missionary preaching (2:1–5). In human terms, the Corinthian church is made up of weak, noninfluential and simple people, whom the world would not reckon as wise. Yet, it was men and women such as they whom God called to be members of Christ and who would reveal God's strength and wisdom. Their weakness parallels that of Christ on the cross, and like the latter they have been chosen to reveal the power of God (1:26–31).

It was no different with Paul, whose preaching and knowledge were void of oratory and philosophy, and who was far from powerful as he came to them in "fear and trembling." Through him, however, God had demonstrated the power of the Spirit. Paul had accepted this and intentionally approached the mission in this way, that no one might mistake human philosophy for the power of God (2:1–5).

STUDY QUESTIONS: Why are factions incompatible with the nature of the Christian community? What is the basic Christian paradox? How does it provide a pattern for understanding Christian life?

MATURE CHRISTIAN WISDOM

6 But still we have a wisdom to offer those who have reached maturity: not a philosophy of our age, it is true, still less of the masters of our age, 7 which are coming to their end. ·The hidden wisdom of God which we teach in our mysteries is the wisdom that God predestined to be for our 8 glory before the ages began. ·It is a wisdom that none of the masters of this age have ever known, or they would not have crucified the Lord of 9 Glory; ·we teach what scripture calls: the things that no eye has seen and no ear has heard, things beyond the mind of man, all that God has prepared for those who love him.

10 These are the very things that God has revealed to us through the Spirit, for the Spirit reaches the depths of everything, even the depths of God. 11 After all, the depths of a man can only be known by his own spirit, not by any other man, and in the same way the depths of God can only be known 12 by the Spirit of God. ·Now instead of the spirit of the world, we have received the Spirit that comes from God, to teach us to understand the gifts that 13 he has given us. ·Therefore we teach, not in the way in which philosophy is taught, but in the way that the Spirit teaches us: we teach spiritual 14 things spiritually. ·An unspiritual person is one who does not accept anything of the Spirit of God: he sees it all as nonsense; it is beyond his understanding because it can only be understood 15 by means of the Spirit. ·A spiritual man, on the other hand, is able to judge the value of everything, and his own value is not to be judged by 16 other men. ·As scripture says: Who can know the

mind of the Lord, so who can teach him? But
we are those who have the mind of Christ.

1 **3** Brothers, I myself was unable to speak to you
as people of the Spirit: I treated you as sen-
2 sual men, still infants in Christ. ·What I fed you
with was milk, not solid food, for you were not
ready for it; and indeed, you are still not ready for
3 it ·since you are still unspiritual. Isn't that obvious
from all the jealousy and wrangling that there is
among you, from the way that you go on behav-
4 ing like ordinary people? ·What could be more
unspiritual than your slogans, "I am for Paul" and
"I am for Apollos?"

☩

Having restated the radical and unchanging basis of
all Christian evangelization, Paul now describes the
wisdom which builds on such a foundation. This wisdom, however, presupposes a considerable degree of
Christian maturity (2:6a), a level of maturity to which
the Corinthians have not yet risen, as is clear from
their present factionalism (3:1–4). They consequently
have no grounds for abandoning Paul and his teaching
and for rallying to Apollos as though the two apostles
and their message were mutually exclusive. The problem lies squarely with the Corinthians, who were not
ready for Paul's presentation of Christian wisdom. Paul
thus defends the apostleship which he had affirmed
from the letter's very first statement (1:1).

The wisdom which Paul offers, like the proclamation
of Jesus crucified, has nothing to do with purely ra-
tional philosophy and its expounders. Such wisdom is
earthbound and temporal (2:6b). Paul's, on the other
hand, is eternal and transcendent, hidden in God's
mystery from all ages. Had the masters of earthly wis-

dom known of this divine wisdom, they would not have
crucified Jesus (2:7–9).

Paul's wisdom is revealed through the Spirit of God.
Just as the depths of man are known only through the
spirit of man, so also with the depths of God which are
known only through the Spirit of God. Accordingly,
the wisdom of God, which bears on the gifts we have
received, can be taught only through the Spirit of God,
and it can be grasped only by those who share in the
life of that Spirit (2:10–16). Although Paul was prepared to teach in this way, the Corinthians were still
far too unspiritual to receive his teaching. They had yet
to rise to the challenge of their calling and to become
in fact what they were in principle and in God's eyes
(3:1–4).

STUDY QUESTIONS: What is the nature of Christian wis-
                 dom? How does it compare with
                 purely human wisdom?

1 Corinthians 3:5–17
COMPLEMENTARY MINISTRIES

⁵ After all, what is Apollos and what is Paul?
They are servants who brought the faith to you.
Even the different ways in which they brought it

⁶ were assigned to them by the Lord. ·I did the
planting, Apollos did the watering, but God made

⁷ things grow. ·Neither the planter nor the waterer

⁸ matters: only God, who makes things grow. ·It
is all one who does the planting and who does the
watering, and each will duly be paid according to

⁹ his share in the work. ·We are fellow workers
with God; you are God's farm, God's building.

¹⁰ By the grace God gave me, I succeeded as an
architect and laid the foundations, on which
someone else is doing the building. Everyone do-

¹¹ ing the building must work carefully. ·For the
foundation, nobody can lay any other than the
one which has already been laid, that is Jesus

¹² Christ. ·On this foundation you can build in gold,
silver and jewels, or in wood, grass and straw,

¹³ but whatever the material, the work of each
builder is going to be clearly revealed when the
day comes. That day will begin with fire, and the

¹⁴ fire will test the quality of each man's work. ·If
his structure stands up to it, he will get his wages;

¹⁵ if it is burned down, he will be the loser, and
though he is saved himself, it will be as one who
has gone through fire.

¹⁶ Didn't you realize that you were God's temple
and that the Spirit of God was living among you?

¹⁷ If anybody should destroy the temple of God,
God will destroy him, because the temple of God
is sacred; and you are that temple.

✠

After describing the situation at Corinth (1:10–16) and presenting the grounds and the rationale for his own apostolic mission (1:17–3:4), Paul clarifies the relationship between his own work and that of Apollos (3:5–17). His purpose is to affirm the importance and complementarity of both. The Corinthians have no grounds for dismissing his foundational contribution and for dividing into factions.

Apollos and Paul are both in the service of the faith, but as servants each had been assigned for a different task (3:5). These tasks are described and related by means of two complex metaphors, one from horticulture (3:6–9) and the other from architecture (3:10–15).

The Corinthian church is God's farm or garden and Paul and Apollos are God's fellow workers on that farm (3:9). Paul's work had been to plant; Apollos came later and watered the garden which Paul had planted (3:6a). The two were obviously complementary and united in one single work (3:8a). There should be no mistaking their role, however. It is God alone who makes things grow (3:6b) and he alone who matters (3:7). He it is who will pay those who had worked on his farm, each according to his part in the common enterprise (3:8b).

In the same way, the Corinthians are God's building (3:9b). Paul himself had laid the foundations of that building, and Apollos and others came later to build on those foundations (3:10a). The latter must work with great care (3:10b), avoiding two pitfalls.

The first would be to replace the foundation which is Jesus Christ (3:11). Paul thus alludes to those who

would set aside his fundamental proclamation of Christ
crucified (1:17-25) which is the basis of all further
development, whether by himself (2:6 – 3:4) or by another such as Apollos (3:5-9).

The second pitfall would be to build with poor materials. Not all building materials are of the same quality.
Paul thus warns his readers that even those who accept
the foundations he has laid could be putting up a building which will one day be revealed as altogether inade-
quate. The day in question is the day of the Lord, a
day of judgment, when fire will test the building's quality. Should the building burn, the builder may be saved,
but he will not be paid for his work (3:12-15). Open
to the ministry of Apollos and others as well-inten-
tioned and good in itself, Paul thus has serious questions about the edifice which they have been raising on
the foundations he had laid. He himself had judged the
Corinthians too immature for the wisdom which these
others had imparted (3:1-4).

Going beyond his general architectural metaphor,
Paul points out that the Corinthian community is God's
temple and the dwelling of God's Spirit (3:16). In so
doing, he abandons the developmental image presented
in 3:10-15 and views the church as an existing sacred
edifice. Should anyone destroy that temple, God himself will destroy him (3:17). Paul's preoccupation has
thus moved away from the relationship between his
work and that of Apollos to address the destructiveness
of various members of the community.

STUDY QUESTIONS: How are the ministry of Paul and
of Apollos related in the Corinthian
mission? In what ways does Paul
use an architectural metaphor?
What is Paul's attitude toward
Apollos?

1 Corinthians 3:18 – 4:21
AN EXAMPLE TO BE IMITATED

¹⁸ Make no mistake about it: if any one of you thinks of himself as wise, in the ordinary sense of the word, then he must learn to be a fool before ¹⁹ he really can be wise. ·Why? Because the wisdom of this world is foolishness to God. As scripture says: The Lord knows wise men's thoughts: he ²⁰ knows how useless they are: ·or again: God is not ²¹ convinced by the arguments of the wise. ·So there is nothing to boast about in anything human: ²² Paul, Apollos, Cephas, the world, life and death, the present and the future, are all your servants; ²³ but you belong to Christ and Christ belongs to God.

¹ 4 People must think of us as Christ's servants, stewards entrusted with the mysteries of God. ² What is expected of stewards is that each one ³ should be found worthy of his trust. ·Not that it makes the slightest difference to me whether you, or indeed any human tribunal, find me worthy or not. I will not even pass judgment on myself. ⁴ True, my conscience does not reproach me at all, but that does not prove that I am acquitted: ⁵ the Lord alone is my judge. ·There must be no passing of premature judgment. Leave that until the Lord comes: he will light up all that is hidden in the dark and reveal the secret intentions of men's hearts. Then will be the time for each one to have whatever praise he deserves from God.

⁶ Now in everything I have said here, brothers, I have taken Apollos and myself as an example (remember the maxim: "Keep to what is written"); it is not for you, so full of your own im-

portance, to go taking sides for one man against
7 another. ·In any case, brother, has anybody given
you some special right? What do you have that
was not given to you? And if it was given, how
8 can you boast as though it were not? ·Is it that
you have everything you want—that you are rich
already, in possession of your kingdom, with us
left outside? Indeed I wish you were really kings,
9 and we could be kings with you! ·But instead, it
seems to me, God has put us apostles at the end
of his parade, with the men sentenced to death; it
is true—we have been put on show in front of the
10 whole universe, angels as well as men. ·Here we
are, fools for the sake of Christ, while you are the
learned men in Christ; we have no power, but
you are influential; you are celebrities, we are
11 nobodies. ·To this day, we go without food and
drink and clothes; we are beaten and have no
12 homes; ·we work for our living with our own
hands. When we are cursed, we answer with a
blessing; when we are hounded, we put up with
13 it; ·we are insulted and we answer politely. We
are treated as the offal of the world, still to this
day, the scum of the earth.
14   I am saying all this not just to make you
ashamed but to bring you, as my dearest chil-
15 dren, to your senses. ·You might have thousands
of guardians in Christ, but not more than one father and it was I who begot you in Christ Jesus by
16 preaching the Good News. ·That is why I beg you
17 to copy me ·and why I have sent you Timothy,
my dear and faithful son in the Lord: he will remind you of the way that I live in Christ, as I
teach it everywhere in all the churches.
18   When it seemed that I was not coming to visit
19 you, some of you became self-important, ·but I
will be visiting you soon, the Lord willing, and
then I shall want to know not what these self-
important people have to say, but what they can
20 do, ·since the kingdom of God is not just words,
21 it is power. ·It is for you to decide: do I come

with a stick in my hand or in a spirit of love and
good will?

☩

Paul now summarizes and concludes his long response to the factioned community at Corinth
(3:18 – 4:13) and adds a final appeal (4:14–21).

First the conclusion reiterates the paradox of the
cross as reflected in the humble status of the Corinthian
Christians and in the servanthood of those who have
worked in their midst, indeed, of all earthly realities,
which are meant to support their relationship to Christ
and through Christ to God. In the case of the Corinthians, his tone is hortatory; with regard to Paul, Apollos
and Cephas, it is declarative (3:18–23).

This is followed by further developments on
the function of servants. Taking up the theme of
3:8,13–15, Paul affirms that God alone has the right to
judge the quality of the service they have received.
Paul's own conscience does not reproach him. If the
Corinthians find him wanting, that is of no real concern
to him. However, they would do better to leave such a
judgment to God when the fullness of his mystery is
finally disclosed (4:1–5).

Finally, Paul's preoccupation with Apollos and himself is intended not merely to rectify the record and to
provide insight into the various conflicts which led to
the present situation. Beyond this, it is meant as an example or model for dealing with difficulties now and in
the future (4:6a).

The factions which arose over Paul and Apollos may
thus be reflected in the tendency of some to reject Stephanas, whom Paul recognizes as a long-standing

leader in the community (16:15–18, 1:16), in favor of
others (4:6b). This present critical situation appears
uppermost in Paul's mind. Already in 3:12–15 and
3:17 we had sensed how Paul's attention reached past
the work of Apollos to more recent work and dangers.
To facilitate a good Christian resolution, Paul concludes with a diatribe, rapid-fire questions and excla-
mations, whose response is rhetorically assumed and
which bring out the irony in attitudes which elevate the
community far beyond the apostle who had served it
(4:7–13).

In a final appeal, Paul reaffirms his intention, which
is not to shame the Christians but to bring them to
their senses (4:14). To this end, Paul had sent Timothy to Corinth. He would remind the community of
Paul's way and teaching (4:14–17). Paul himself will
soon come to visit them, hopefully, if the present letter
and Timothy's visit have any effect, in a spirit of love
and goodwill. Those who think themselves important
will be judged on their deeds and not on their words
alone (4:18–21).

STUDY QUESTIONS: What is Paul's main purpose in dis-
                  cussing Apollos and himself? What
                  is meant by a diatribe, and how does
                  Paul use it in this passage?

PURIFICATION AND JUDGMENT

¹ 5 I have been told as an undoubted fact that one of you is living with his father's wife. This is a case of sexual immorality among you that must be unparalleled even among pagans. ² How can you be so proud of yourselves? You should be in mourning. A man who does a thing like that ought to have been expelled from the ³ community. ·Though I am far away in body, I am with you in spirit, and have already condemned the man who did this thing as if I were ⁴ actually present. ·When you are assembled together in the name of the Lord Jesus, and I am spiritually present with you, then with the power ⁵ of our Lord Jesus ·he is to be handed over to Satan so that his sensual body may be destroyed and his spirit saved on the day of the Lord.

⁶ The pride that you take in yourselves is hardly to your credit. You must know how even a small amount of yeast is enough to leaven all the dough, ⁷ so get rid of all the old yeast, and make yourselves into a completely new batch of bread, unleavened as you are meant to be. Christ, our passover, has ⁸ been sacrificed; ·let us celebrate the feast, then, by getting rid of all the old yeast of evil and wickedness, having only the unleavened bread of sincerity and truth.

⁹ When I wrote in my letter to you not to asso-
¹⁰ ciate with people living immoral lives, ·I was not meaning to include all the people in the world who are sexually immoral, any more than I meant to include all usurers and swindlers or idol worshipers. To do that, you would have to withdraw
¹¹ from the world altogether. ·What I wrote was that

you should not associate with a brother Christian
who is leading an immoral life, or is a usurer, or
idolatrous, or a slanderer, or a drunkard, or is
dishonest; you should not even eat a meal with
12 people like that. ·It is not my business to pass
judgment on those outside. Of those who are in-
13 side, you can surely be the judges. ·But of those
who are outside, God is the judge.

You must drive out this evildoer from among
you.

✠

A particular case of immorality (5:1) is dealt with
(5:2–5) and provides a springboard for general teaching concerning immorality in the community (5:6–8)
and an important distinction between the apostolic mission and pastoral care (5:9–13). Throughout the unit,
the writer's concern is with the community and not
with the immoral person as such.

The case in question involves a man who is living
with his father's wife, that is with his stepmother. According to Jewish and Roman law, as with ancient
Greek practice, such a union was forbidden as incestuous, and this is reflected in Paul's opening statement
(5:1). Apparently, however, the Corinthian community has done nothing about the matter. From the Corinthian point of view, it may be that the man's father
was not a Christian and that the question of divorce and
marriage remained ethically ambiguous. Later, Paul
would deal with this matter in more general terms
(7:12–16). More probably, however, those who
thought they were in possession of the kingdom
(4:8,19–20) considered themselves beyond the law
and free to do anything. In 6:12, Paul cites a slogan to
this effect and feels compelled to draw an important

distinction in its application. Be that as it may, the situation is judged reprehensible and a sharp contradiction in the face of the community's prideful attitude. Such a man should have been expelled from the community (5:2).

The Corinthians should now proceed to dismiss the man. The appropriate context for such action is the Lord's assembly, when the community acts with the power of the Lord Jesus and when Paul is spiritually present with them. Paul views himself absent in body but spiritually present (1 Co 5:3–4; 1 Th 2:17) to those whom he has begotten in Christ Jesus (1 Co 4:15; 1 Th 2:7,11). The purpose of the dismissal is not that the man be ultimately condemned but that he be open to salvation. He was not a true Christian, able to evangelize others. Outside the community, he would once again be open to the Gospel and the call of Christ.

To appreciate such a stance, we must be able to prescind from later developments in the theological understanding of baptism. In Paul's time, the question of the indissoluble effects of baptism and of its indelible character had not yet surfaced and been resolved. Further, the apostolic and missionary thrust of a church had not yet ceded its primacy to internal pastoral concerns. One was not a Christian for one's own sake but for others, and a Christian had to present the image of Christ to the world.

Just as a little yeast affects all the dough, so with the Christian community. The yeast in this case refers, not to the incestuous member of the community, but to the community's attitude and behavior with regard to immorality (5:6). It must consequently rid itself of such yeast. At this point, a second metaphor is introduced, that of the old yeast which is as inconsistent with the life of the community as the unleavened bread. Prior to its call, the community had been leavened by evil and wickedness. By virtue of Christ's Passover sacrifice, however, it had become an unleavened bread of sincerity and truth, in which there was to be no trace of its former state (5:7–8).

The metaphor becomes clear when we recall how bread was leavened by mixing in some dough from the previous day's batch. On the feast of Passover and Unleavened Bread, a feast celebrating the new harvest, no wheat from the previous year's harvest was used. After Jesus' death-resurrection or Passover, this symbolic practice acquired Christian significance and referred to the new life and challenge of those who were converted from their old ways and joined Jesus in the Passover of Christian life.

From 5:9, we conclude that Paul had written a previous letter to the church at Corinth. In that letter he had apparently spoken in apodictic terms, making no distinction between those outside the community and those inside. At least by some, Paul's injunction not to associate with people living immoral lives must have been taken at its word and absolutely, with the result that it could be set aside as impossible. How could they avoid all immoral persons without removing themselves altogether from the greater world of Corinth? Further, if Paul's statement did not apply to their dealings with outsiders, why should they be concerned with immoral living on the part of insiders?

Responding to the way his letter had been received and interpreted, Paul now clarifies his earlier statement. His concern had been with how to deal with an immoral brother Christian. Such a one should have no part in the Christian solidarity expressed in their fellowship meals. Paul's letter had thus been pastoral,

aimed at the community's internal problems. In no way
did he mean to remove them from the world in which
they had an apostolic missionary function. Nor was it
his business to judge outsiders. God himself would
judge those who did not become Christians (5:9–13).

STUDY QUESTIONS: Why does Paul ask that the Christian who is living with his father's
wife be dismissed from the community? How does his theology of
baptism influence his position?
What is the meaning of yeast in
Paul's metaphorical usage?

1 Corinthians 6:1–8
RESOLVING COMMUNITY CONFLICTS

¹ 6 How dare one of your members take up a complaint against another in the law courts of ² the unjust instead of before the saints? ·As you know, it is the saints who are to "judge the world"; and if the world is to be judged by you, ³ how can you be unfit to judge trifling cases? ·Since we are also to judge angels, it follows that we can ⁴ judge matters of everyday life; ·but when you have had cases of that kind, the people you appointed to try them were not even respected in ⁵ the Church. ·You should be ashamed: is there really not one reliable man among you to settle differences between brothers ·and so one brother ⁶ brings a court case against another in front of ⁷ unbelievers? ·It is bad enough for you to have lawsuits at all against one another: oughtn't you to let yourselves be wronged, and let yourselves ⁸ be cheated? ·But you are doing the wronging and the cheating, and to your own brothers.

✠

The case addressed in 5:1–13 had led to the statement that Christians were to judge those inside the community not those who were outside. By association, this distinction led to a second case, which involved bringing a lawsuit against a fellow Christian in a non-Christian court. Paul thus provides important reflections on the internal affairs of a church in relation to the secular world in which it lives. Note that the matter did not involve a case brought against a Christian by one who was not a Christian, but a case between Christians.

In 6:1–6, Paul upbraids the community for bringing cases for judgment before unrighteous or unbelieving judges. With a series of questions, reflecting the rhetorical style of the diatribe, he means to raise their consciousness concerning their ability and responsibility to settle their own disputes. If one day they are to judge the world, a fortiori they should be able to judge small differences among themselves. Perhaps earlier he had not meant to shame them (4:14). In the present matter, however, he spares no effort to do so (6:5). Paul's views on resolving internal community conflicts and grievances may have been influenced by his experience of Jewish life, where internal matters were settled by Jewish courts.

Such lawsuits do not reflect the attitude of Christians, who should allow themselves to be wronged (6:7). To appreciate this position, we should recall Paul's earlier statements concerning the manifestation of God's glory and power through the cross of Christ, the low estate of the Christians and Paul's own weakness (1:17 – 2:5). However, not only do the Christians reject being wronged; they are actually engaged in wronging and cheating their own brother Christians (6:8).

STUDY QUESTIONS: Why does Paul ask the Christians to resolve their own conflicts without bringing them before civil authorities? How is his position related to the theology of the cross?

1 Corinthians 6:9–20
IMMORALITY: A CHRISTIAN CONTRADICTION

⁹ You know perfectly well that people who do wrong will not inherit the kingdom of God: people of immoral lives, idolaters, adulterers, cata-¹⁰ mites, sodomites, ·thieves, usurers, drunkards, slanderers and swindlers will never inherit the ¹¹ kingdom of God. ·These are the sort of people some of you were once, but now you have been washed clean, and sanctified, and justified through the name of the Lord Jesus Christ and through the Spirit of our God.

¹² "For me there are no forbidden things"; maybe, but not everything does good. I agree there are no forbidden things for me, but I am ¹³ not going to let anything dominate me. ·Food is only meant for the stomach, and the stomach for food; yes, and God is going to do away with both of them. But the body—this is not meant for fornication; it is for the Lord, and the Lord for the ¹⁴ body. ·God, who raised the Lord from the dead, will by his power raise us up too.

¹⁵ You know, surely, that your bodies are members making up the body of Christ; do you think I can take parts of Christ's body and join them to ¹⁶ the body of a prostitute? Never! ·As you know, a man who goes with a prostitute is one body with her, since the two, as it is said, become one flesh. ¹⁷ But anyone who is joined to the Lord is one spirit with him.

¹⁸ Keep away from fornication. All the other sins are committed outside the body; but to fornicate ¹⁹ is to sin against your own body. ·Your body, you know, is the temple of the Holy Spirit, who is in

you since you received him from God. You are
20 not your own property; •You have been bought
and paid for. That is why you should use your
body for the glory of God.

✠

Just as the question of judgment in 5:12–13 had led
to 6:1–8, these last verses, which ended on the theme
of wronging one's brothers, lead to 6:9–20, which deal
with doing wrong in general (6:9–11) and with sexual
immorality in particular (6:12–20). The latter focus
was occasioned by the case of incest presented in
5:1–13.

To describe immoral persons, Paul draws on a cata-
logue of vices which was traditional and familiar in the
Greek world of Stoic philosophy and education. The
same had influenced Paul in 5:10–11. In so doing, he
means to evoke the pre-Christian life of his readers,
who had once been sinners even in the eyes of the
Greek world from which they came to Christ. Such immoral persons will not inherit the kingdom of God.
Having been washed clean, sanctified and justified, the
Christians should act according to their new Christian
nature (6:9–11).

The Corinthians were apparently using a popular
Christian slogan to justify sexual immorality: "For me
there are no forbidden things," which can also be translated "I am free to do anything" (6:12a). Such a slogan might well have developed from Paul's own teaching on freedom in Christ. For the Corinthians, it must
have been associated with the view that they were already in full possession of the kingdom (4:8,19–20).
Hence Paul's insistence that those who do such things
would not inherit the kingdom (6:9–10). The same

slogan was used to justify the eating of meat which had
been offered to idols (10:23). Like so many slogans,
however, its application was far from universal. While
accepting it, Paul points out that Christians are not free
to do things which dominate them and take away their
freedom (6:12b). As earlier in the matter of associating with persons leading immoral lives (5:9–13), Paul
thus finds it necessary to draw a distinction.

A second slogan was being used to buttress the first:
"Food is only for the stomach, and the stomach for
food." Paul agrees and adds further that "God is going
to do away with both of them." However, since the
body is for the Lord and the Lord for the body, the
slogan does not justify sexual immorality. Unlike the
stomach, the body will be raised from the dead, just as
the Lord had been raised (6:13–14). At this point,
Paul prescinds from matters which pertain strictly to
food. These will be taken up in 10:23–30.

In the present context, the general term *porneia,*
which refers to sexual immorality, applies more
specifically to sexual relations with a prostitute. Such
relations are not consistent with a Christian's union in
one spirit with Christ (6:15–17). Those who form one
body in Christ must not form one flesh or body with a
prostitute. Paul concludes the unit by repeating his
teaching on the Christian community as the temple of
the Holy Spirit. A body which is God's dwelling must
be used for God's glory (6:18–20).

STUDY QUESTIONS: How did the Corinthians justify
sexual immorality? What is the
meaning of *porneia,* and why does
Paul deem it wrong?

1 Corinthians 7:1 – 16:24
A LETTER FROM CORINTH

In the second part of the letter, Paul deals primarily with various questions (7:1,25, 8:1, 12:1, 16:1) included in a letter which was sent to him from Corinth. However, he also comments on at least one statement made in that letter (11:2), and he no doubt was influenced by the verbal report of those who had brought it on behalf of the community, namely Stephanas, Fortunatus and Achaicus (16:17).

Responding to the first three questions, Paul discusses and provides concrete guidelines for marriage and sexuality (7:1–24), celibacy (7:25–40), and eating food sacrificed to idols (8:1 – 11:1). The third question had called for some reflections on the Lord's Supper (10:14–22) and this invited a long discussion on order in the assembly (11:2 – 14:40).

Beginning with comments on a Corinthian statement concerning fidelity to tradition (11:2–34), Paul proceeds to answer the fourth question, which deals with spiritual gifts (12:1 – 14:40). Before taking up the fifth and final question concerning the collection for needy communities (16:1–4), Paul inserts a long development on the resurrection of Christians (15:1–58). As earlier in the letter, his concern is to affirm the grounds of tradition and to develop its implications for belief and practice.

Judging by its position in the letter and the careful

attention it receives, the question of faith in the resurrection must have been viewed as an important key to resolving all the other problems which plagued the Corinthian community.

1 Corinthians 7:1-40
MARRIAGE, SEXUALITY AND CELIBACY

¹ 7 Now for the questions about which you wrote. Yes, it is a good thing for a man not to touch ² a woman; ·but since sex is always a danger, let each man have his own wife and each woman her ³ own husband. ·The husband must give his wife what she has the right to expect, and so too the ⁴ wife to the husband. ·The wife has no rights over her own body; it is the husband who has them. In the same way, the husband has no rights over ⁵ his body; the wife has them. ·Do not refuse each other except by mutual consent, and then only for an agreed time, to leave yourselves free for prayer; then come together again in case Satan should take advantage of your weakness to tempt ⁶/⁷ you. ·This is a suggestion, not a rule: ·I should like everyone to be like me, but everybody has his own particular gifts from God, one with a gift for one thing and another with a gift for the opposite.

⁸ There is something I want to add for the sake of widows and those who are not married: it is a good thing for them to stay as they are, like me, ⁹ but if they cannot control the sexual urges, they should get married, since it is better to be married than to be tortured.

¹⁰ For the married I have something to say, and this is not from me but from the Lord: a wife ¹¹ must not leave her husband—·or if she does leave him, she must either remain unmarried or else make it up with her husband—nor must a husband send his wife away.

¹² The rest is from me and not from the Lord. If a brother has a wife who is an unbeliever, and she

is content to live with him, he must not send her
13 away; ·and if a woman has an unbeliever for her
husband, and he is content to live with her, she
14 must not leave him. ·This is because the unbelieving husband is made one with the saints
through his wife, and the unbelieving wife is
made one with the saints through her husband.
If this were not so, your children would be un-
15 clean, whereas in fact they are holy. ·However, if
the unbelieving partner does not consent, they
may separate; in these circumstances, the brother
or sister is not tied: God has called you to a life
16 of peace. ·If you are a wife, it may be your part
to save your husband, for all you know; if a husband, for all you know, it may be your part to
save your wife.
17 For the rest, what each one has is what the
Lord has given him and he should continue as he
was when God's call reached him. This is the rul-
18 ing that I give in all the churches. ·If anyone had
already been circumcised at the time of his call,
he need not disguise it, and anyone who was un-
circumcised at the time of his call need not be
19 circumcised; ·because to be circumcised or un-
circumcised means nothing: what does matter is
20 to keep the commandments of God. ·Let everyone
21 stay as he was at the time of his call. ·If, when
you were called, you were a slave, do not let this
bother you; but if you should have the chance of
22 being free, accept it. ·A slave, when he is called
in the Lord, becomes the Lord's freedman, and
a freeman called in the Lord becomes Christ's
23 slave. ·You have all been bought and paid for; do
24 not be slaves of other men. ·Each one of you, my
brothers, should stay as he was before God at the
time of his call.
25 About remaining celibate, I have no direc-
tions from the Lord but give my own opinion as
one who, by the Lord's mercy, has stayed faith-
26 ful. ·Well then, I believe that in these present
times of stress this is right: that it is good for a

27 man to stay as he is. ·If you are tied to a wife, do not look for freedom; if you are free of a wife,
28 then do not look for one. ·But if you marry, it is no sin, and it is not a sin for a young girl to get married. They will have their troubles, though, in their married life, and I should like to spare you that.

29   Brothers, this is what I mean: our time is growing short. Those who have wives should live
30 as though they had none, ·and those who mourn should live as though they had nothing to mourn for; those who are enjoying life should live as though there were nothing to laugh about; those whose life is buying things should live as though
31 they had nothing of their own; ·and those who have to deal with the world should not become engrossed in it. I say this because the world as we know it is passing away.

32   I would like to see you free from all worry. An unmarried man can devote himself to the Lord's affairs, all he need worry about is pleasing the
33 Lord; ·but a married man has to bother about the world's affairs and devote himself to pleasing his
34 wife: ·he is torn two ways. In the same way an unmarried woman, like a young girl, can devote herself to the Lord's affairs; all she need worry about is being holy in body and spirit. The married woman, on the other hand, has to worry about the world's affairs and devote herself to
35 pleasing her husband. ·I say this only to help you, not to put a halter around your necks, but simply to make sure that everything is as it should be, and that you give your undivided attention to the Lord.

36   Still, if there is anyone who feels that it would not be fair to his daughter to let her grow too old for marriage, and that he should do something about it, he is free to do as he likes: he is not
37 sinning if there is a marriage. ·On the other hand, if someone has firmly made his mind up, without any compulsion and in complete freedom of

choice, to keep his daughter as she is, he will be
38 doing a good thing. ·In other words, the man who
sees that his daughter is married has done a good
thing but the man who keeps his daughter unmarried has done something even better.

39   A wife is tied as long as her husband is alive.
But if the husband dies, she is free to marry any-
40 body she likes, only it must be in the Lord. ·She
would be happier, in my opinion, if she stayed as
she is—and I too have the Spirit of God, I think.

✠

The first two questions in the letter which Paul received from Corinth concern marriage and sexual relations (7:1) and celibacy (7:25). Three points should
be noted concerning Paul's responses (7:1–24,25–40)
to these questions. First he is careful to apply his general teaching to various situations and specific cases.
He thus forestalls possible misunderstanding such as
had occurred over his previous letter (5:9–13). Second
he distinguishes between teaching which was from the
Lord (7:10) and teaching for which he assumes personal responsibility (7:12) as one who is faithful
(7:25) and has the Spirit of God (7:40). Third, while
excluding sexual immorality (*porneia*), he does not
mean to impose restrictions in the area of marriage but
to temper the tendency to do so. Exaggerated asceticism
was no more acceptable than libertinism.

From Paul's reply, we must assume that some of the
Corinthians favored sexual abstinence for all but that
this view was not altogether clear or accepted. Paul responds that in principle "it is a good thing for a man
not to touch a woman" (7:1), but that this does not in
the concrete preclude marriage and marital relations.

Not all are gifted in the same way. Some are divinely gifted to be celibate, as indeed he was, while others are gifted to marry (7:7b), and this reality takes precedence over Paul's personal preference (7:7a). In 7:2–6, he provides married Christians with pastoral guidance for discerning appropriate behavior in their sexual relationship.

After this general introductory statement (7:1–7), guidelines are provided for widows and the unmarried (7:8–9), for married Christians (7:10–11) and for married couples which include an unbelieving (non-Christian) partner (7:12–16). In each case, Paul's general principle is that Christians should remain in the state of life, whether married or unmarried, which was theirs at the time of their calling. This principle is thrice repeated in 7:17–24, where Paul broadens the context to include other areas to which the same applies.

The reason for Paul's position that each should stay as he is at the time of his call becomes clear as he takes up the question concerning celibacy (7:25). Christians are living in the time of stress (7:26), a time which is growing short (7:29) and which calls for undivided attention to the affairs of the Lord (7:32–35). Paul's position that celibacy is preferable to marriage in cases where someone is still single (7:27,38) or has become widowed (7:40) is thus contingent on the view that history was fast coming to an end. There was consequently no point to change one's state of life, unless this proved personally and ethically necessary. The Lord's imminent coming called for full and undivided attention.

The translation of 7:36–38, which here governs the role of a father in the marriage of his daughter, is disputed. More probably, Paul is referring to a couple which was engaged at the time of their calling.

STUDY QUESTIONS: What general principle governs Paul's positions on marriage? How is this principle related to his view of history? Is Paul's position valid for the Church today?

1 Corinthians 8:1 – 9:27
SENSITIVITY FOR THE WEAK

8 ¹ Now about food sacrificed to idols. "We all have knowledge"; yes, that is so, but knowledge gives self-importance—it is love that makes ² the building grow. ·A man may imagine he understands something, but still not understand any-³ thing in the way that he ought to. ·But any man ⁴ who loves God is known by him. ·Well then, about eating food sacrificed to idols: we know that idols do not really exist in the world and that ⁵ there is no god but the One. ·And even if there were things called gods, either in the sky or on earth—where there certainly seem to be "gods" ⁶ and "lords" in plenty—still for us there is one God, the Father from whom all things come and for whom we exist; and there is one Lord, Jesus Christ, through whom all things come and through whom we exist.

⁷ Some people, however, do not have this knowledge. There are some who have been so long used to idols that they eat this food as though it really had been sacrificed to the idol, and their con-⁸ science, being weak, is defiled by it. ·Food, of course, cannot bring us in touch with God: we lose nothing if we refuse to eat, we gain nothing ⁹ if we eat. ·Only be careful that you do not make use of this freedom in a way that proves a pitfall ¹⁰ for the weak. ·Suppose someone sees you, a man who understands, eating in some temple of an idol; his own conscience, even if it is weak, may encourage him to eat food which has been offered ¹¹ to idols. ·In this way your knowledge could become the ruin of someone weak, of a brother for ¹² whom Christ died. ·By sinning in this way against

your brothers, and injuring their weak consciences, it would be Christ against whom you
¹³ sinned. ·That is why, since food can be the occasion of my brother's downfall, I shall never eat
meat again in case I am the cause of a brother's
downfall.

¹ 9 I, personally, am free: I am an apostle and I
have seen Jesus our Lord. You are all my
² work in the Lord. ·Even if I were not an apostle
to others, I should still be an apostle to you who
³ are the seal of my apostolate in the Lord. ·My
answer to those who want to interrogate me is
⁴ this: ·Have we not every right to eat and drink?
⁵ And the right to take a Christian woman around
with us, like all the other apostles and the brothers
⁶ of the Lord and Cephas? ·Are Barnabas and I
the only ones who are not allowed to stop work-
⁷ ing? ·Nobody ever paid money to stay in the
army, and nobody ever planted a vineyard and
refused to eat the fruit of it. Who has there ever
been that kept a flock and did not feed on the
milk from his flock?

⁸   These may be only human comparisons, but
⁹ does not the Law itself say the same thing? ·It is
written in the Law of Moses: You must not put a
muzzle on the ox when it is treading out the corn.
¹⁰ Is it about oxen that God is concerned, ·or is there
not an obvious reference to ourselves? Clearly
this was written for our sake to show that the
plowman ought to plow in expectation, and the
thresher to thresh in the expectation of getting
¹¹ his share. ·If we have sown spiritual things for
you, why should you be surprised if we harvest
¹² your material things? ·Others are allowed these
rights over you and our right is surely greater? In
fact we have never exercised this right. On the
contrary we have put up with anything rather
than obstruct the Good News of Christ in any
¹³ way. ·Remember that the ministers serving in the
Temple get their food from the Temple and those
serving at the altar can claim their share from the

¹⁴ altar itself. ·In the same sort of way the Lord directed that those who preach the gospel should get their living from the gospel.

¹⁵   However, I have not exercised any of these rights, and I am not writing all this to secure this treatment for myself. I would rather die than let anyone take away something that I can boast of. ¹⁶ Not that I do boast of preaching the gospel, since it is a duty which has been laid on me; I should ¹⁷ be punished if I did not preach it! ·If I had chosen this work myself, I might have been paid for it, but as I have not, it is a responsibility which has ¹⁸ been put into my hands. ·Do you know what my reward is? It is this: in my preaching, to be able to offer the Good News free, and not insist on the rights which the gospel gives me.

¹⁹   So though I am not a slave of any man I have made myself the slave of everyone so as to win as ²⁰ many as I could. ·I made myself a Jew to the Jews, to win the Jews; that is, I who am not a subject of the Law made myself a subject of the Law to those who are the subjects of the Law, to win ²¹ those who are subject to the Law. ·To those who have no Law, I was free of the Law myself (though not free from God's law, being under the law of Christ) to win those who have no Law. ²² For the weak I made myself weak. I made myself all things to all men in order to save some at any ²³ cost; ·and I still do this, for the sake of the gospel, to have a share in its blessings.

²⁴   All the runners at the stadium are trying to win, but only one of them gets the prize. You ²⁵ must run in the same way, meaning to win. ·All the fighters at the games go into strict training; they do this just to win a wreath that will wither away, but we do it for a wreath that will never ²⁶ wither. ·That is how I run, intent on winning; that ²⁷ is how I fight, not beating the air. ·I treat my body hard and make it obey me, for, having been an announcer myself, I should not want to be disqualified.

✠

Paul now takes up a third question about which the community had written, that of eating food which had been sacrificed to idols (8:1a). His response extends from 8:1 to 11:1.

There were those in the community who maintained that they had full freedom in this matter since they were in possession of Christian knowledge (*gnosis*) and knew that idols had no objective reality (8:1,4). Their claim that "we all have knowledge" (8:1) is related to the slogan "For me there are no forbidden things" (6:12; 10:23) and parallels a Corinthian position on sexuality which Paul addressed in 6:12–14.

On the other hand, there were others whose attitude towards idols was at best ambivalent and for whom eating food offered to idols could hardly be considered innocent or indifferent (8:7). Writing to all, and aware that both tendencies were represented in the one community, Paul addresses the various issues related to each of these groups. In so doing, however, he never loses sight of their relationship to one another and of their influence on one another in the one body of Christ (8:9–13). Since the greater influence was apt to be exerted by the "strong" members of the community, it is they who constitute his principal preoccupation in 8:1–11:1.

In his response, Paul points first to the dangers of knowledge when it is divorced from love. Drawing once again on his developmental metaphor from architecture (3:10–15), he emphasizes the role of love in the building's growth (8:1b). Without love, knowledge is vitiated (8:2–3), a theme which will be developed more amply in 13:1–13.

Second, Paul agrees that idols have no reality and that there is only one God. However, even if some realities could be termed "gods" or "lords," the fact remains that for Christians there is but one God and one Lord, Jesus Christ. Such discussions should not be allowed to cloud the issue (8:4–6).

The problem, however, lies not so much in the knowledge of those who have written to Paul (8:1–6) as in the fact that some do not have this knowledge (8:7–13). In principle, eating food which had been offered to idols is indifferent (8:8), and the Corinthians are indeed free. However, freedom has its limits. Just as they were not free to abdicate their freedom (6:12), neither are they free to bring about the downfall of weak, brother Christians, who in practice do not share this knowledge concerning the nothingness of idols.

Paul's own freedom and the way he uses it in concrete situations provides a good model or example of behavior for the Corinthians (9:1–27). In 1:10–4:21, Paul's relationship to Apollos in the evangelization of Corinth had provided a similar model. Paul has not taken advantage of his rights and freedom as an apostle, especially in matters of physical sustenance (9:1–18). Rather his whole life was governed by the concrete demands of service to others for the sake of the Gospel (9:19–23). Rather than focus on one's freedom, one must direct all one's efforts to reaching life's goal by being of service to others (9:24–27). For Corinthians accustomed to athletic contests in the marketplace, Paul's metaphors from the games provide vivid illustrations.

STUDY QUESTIONS: How is the Corinthians' stand on eating food sacrificed to idols related to their position on sexual morality? What principles does Paul use to solve the moral dilemma?

1 Corinthians 10:1 – 11:1
SALVATION NOT AUTOMATIC

¹ **10** I want to remind you, brothers, how our fathers were all guided by a cloud above them and how they all passed through the sea. ² They were all baptized into Moses in this cloud ³ and in this sea; ·all ate the same spiritual food ⁴ and all drank the same spiritual drink, since they all drank from the spiritual rock that followed them as they went, and that rock was Christ. ⁵ In spite of this, most of them failed to please God and their corpses littered the desert.

⁶ These things all happened as warnings for us, not to have the wicked lusts for forbidden things ⁷ that they had. ·Do not become idolaters as some of them did, for scripture says: After sitting down to eat and drink, the people got up to amuse ⁸ themselves. ·We must never fall into sexual immorality: some of them did, and twenty-three ⁹ thousand met their downfall in one day. ·We are not to put the Lord to the test: some of them ¹⁰ did, and they were killed by snakes. ·You must never complain: some of them did, and they were killed by the Destroyer.

¹¹ All this happened to them as a warning, and it was written down to be a lesson for us who are ¹² living at the end of the age. ·The man who thinks he is safe must be careful that he does not fall. ¹³ The trials that you have had to bear are no more than people normally have. You can trust God not to let you be tried beyond your strength, and with any trial he will give you a way out of it and the strength to bear it.

¹⁴ This is the reason, my dear brothers, why you ¹⁵ must keep clear of idolatry. ·I say to you as sen-

sible people: judge for yourselves what I am
16 saying. ·The blessing cup that we bless is a communion with the blood of Christ, and the bread
that we break is a communion with the body of
17 Christ. ·The fact that there is only one loaf means
that, though there are many of us, we form a
single body because we all have a share in this
18 one loaf. ·Look at the other Israel, the race, where
those who eat the sacrifices are in communion
19 with the altar. ·Does this mean that the food sacrificed to idols has a real value, or that the idol
20 itself is real? ·Not at all. It simply means that the
sacrifices that they offer they sacrifice to demons
who are not God. I have no desire to see you in
21 communion with demons. ·You cannot drink the
cup of the Lord and the cup of demons. You
cannot take your share at the table of the Lord
22 and at the table of demons. ·Do we want to make
the Lord angry; are we stronger than he is?

23   "For me there are no forbidden things," but
not everything does good. True, there are no forbidden things, but it is not everything that helps
24 the building to grow. ·Nobody should be looking
for his own advantage, but everybody for the
25 other man's. ·Do not hesitate to eat anything that
is sold in butchers' shops: there is no need to raise
26 questions of conscience; ·for the earth and every-
27 thing that is in it belong to the Lord. ·If an unbeliever invites you to his house, go if you want
to, and eat whatever is put in front of you, without asking questions just to satisfy conscience.
28 But if someone says to you, "This food was offered in sacrifice," then, out of consideration for
the man that told you, you should not eat it, for
29 the sake of his scruples; ·his scruples, you see,
not your own. Why should my freedom depend
30 on somebody else's conscience? ·If I take my
share with thankfulness, why should I be blamed
for food for which I have thanked God?

31   Whatever you eat, whatever you drink, whatever you do at all, do it for the glory of God.
32 Never do anything offensive to anyone—to Jews

³³ or Greeks or to the Church of God; ·just as I try
to be helpful to everyone at all times, not anxious
for my own advantage but for the advantage of
everybody else, so that they may be saved.

11 ¹ Take me for your model, as I take
Christ.

✠

In 9:1–27, Paul's own life and behavior provided a
model for resolving the question of eating food which
had been sacrificed to idols (8:1–13). He now supplements his argument by developing precedents from the
biblical history of the Exodus (10:1–13). The same
examples provide the point of departure for the argument in 10:14–22 where Paul's attention focuses primarily on the weak members of the community, to
whom he had referred in 8:7.

As in 8:1 – 9:27, Paul's purpose is not only to instruct but to exhort. Beginning with 10:1, however, his
exhortation takes the form of a warning. The Christians should not think that just because they are united
in partaking of the body and blood of Christ
(10:16–17) they will automatically be saved. Their fathers had enjoyed a kind of Mosaic baptism, eaten a
spiritual food and been led by a spiritual rock which
was actually Christ (10:1–4). However, since they
then proceeded to engage in idol worship and sexual
immorality as well as to test God and complain, they
died (10:5–10). All this happened as a warning, first
to their fathers (10:11–12) and now to them (10:6).
They are being tried, but they can be sure that God
will not try them beyond their strength (10:13). The
struggle and effort of the Corinthians (9:24–27) is

thus viewed from the standpoint of God's activity on their behalf.

For the "weak" Christians, all of this means that they should not engage in idolatrous sacrificial banquets. Even if the idol, and the food sacrificed to it, is nothing in itself, to engage in such activities is to remove oneself from the fellowship which they enjoy in Christ's body and blood. Sharing in an idolatrous table is demonic and incompatible with the table of the Lord (10:14–22).

In conclusion, Paul then summarizes his statements on the limits of Christian freedom (6:12, 9:1) and appeals to the community to be sensitive to the needs and the salvation of others. Besides their own conscience, that of others must always be carefully considered (10:23–33). In resolving concrete practical questions, let Paul be their model as Christ is his (11:1).

Paul thus concludes his lengthy response to the third question (8:1–11:1) with a reiteration of the important principle of Pauline imitation, a principle already given in 1 Th 1:6, 2 Th 3:7–9 and 1 Co 4:16. In 8:1–11:1, and on numerous previous occasions, Paul had applied this principle by appealing to his life, attitude and behavior as a model to be followed. The principle consequently functions as a summary statement of one of the fundamental elements in primary evangelization and in the process of Christianity's historical transmission.

STUDY QUESTIONS: What is the point of Paul's biblical argument concerning baptism and Eucharist? Is Christian freedom an absolute and unlimited prerogative?

1 Corinthians 11:2–16
FIDELITY TO CUSTOM

2 You have done well in remembering me so constantly and in maintaining the traditions just
3 as I passed them on to you. ·However, what I want you to understand is that Christ is the head of every man, man is the head of woman, and
4 God is the head of Christ. ·For a man to pray or prophesy with his head covered is a sign of dis-
5 respect to his head. ·For a woman, however, it is a sign of disrespect to her head if she prays or prophesies unveiled; she might as well have her
6 hair shaved off. ·In fact, a woman who will not wear a veil ought to have her hair cut off. If a woman is ashamed to have her hair cut off or shaved, she ought to wear a veil.

7 A man should certainly not cover his head, since he is the image of God and reflects God's glory; but woman is the reflection of man's glory.
8 For man did not come from woman; no, woman
9 came from man; ·and man was not created for for the sake of woman, but woman was created
10 for the sake of man. ·That is the argument for women's covering their heads with a symbol of the authority over them, out of respect for the
11 angels. ·However, though woman cannot do without man, neither can man do without woman, in
12 the Lord; ·woman may come from man, but man is born of woman—both come from God.

13 Ask yourselves if it is fitting for a woman to
14 pray to God without a veil; ·and whether nature itself does not tell you that long hair on a man is
15 nothing to be admired, ·while a woman, who was given her hair as a covering, thinks long hair her glory?

16   To anyone who might still want to argue: it is
not the custom with us, nor in the churches of
God.

✠

In their letter, the Corinthians had submitted a number of questions and Paul responded to three of these
in 7:1–24,25–40; 8:1 – 11:1. The letter, however, was
not limited to questions. From 11:2 we conclude that
they had also affirmed their fidelity in maintaining the
traditions as Paul had passed them on to them. Paul
commends them for this in this introductory verse
which allows us to see the close link between the notion of tradition and the imitation of Paul (11:1). The
latter represents the process through which the traditions are actually maintained.

The question of tradition is fundamental in the subsequent chapters where Paul appeals to customary
practice (11:16) as well as to early liturgical (11:
23–25) and creedal (15:3–5) formulas for discerning appropriate Christian behavior and belief in related areas. In chapters 11–14, Paul addresses various
problems concerning the Christian assembly. Their assumption at this point was suggested by the discussion
concerning the table of the Lord in 10:14–22. As in
1:10 – 6:20, the order is thus determined by association of subject matter and themes. In chapter 15, Paul
takes up the fundamental matter of the resurrection of
Christians.

While affirming their fidelity to the traditions, the
Corinthians must also have presented a number of
problems which had arisen in the process. One of these
concerned the relationship between men and women in

120 FIDELITY TO CUSTOM

the assembly. The fact that both took part in the communal prayer and in prophesying (11:4–5,13) had led to a blurring of their social distinction and this was reflected in the way women joined the men in maintaining their heads uncovered. If Paul appears to pay disproportionate attention to the matter of women wearing a veil, it is that he views the latter as a symptom of the broader problems disturbing the assembly and especially of the growing individualism which threatened its unity and harmony.

In 11:2–16, Paul's concern is primarily with Christian decorum in the service of the Word. In 11:17–34, his focus is on the celebration of the Lord's Supper. While the Word and the Supper are treated separately, this does not mean that the liturgy had already developed into the ordered structure represented in the liturgy of the Word and the eucharistic meal. Prayer and prophesying may have begun before the actual meal but they continued during the course of the meal and even after its conclusion. The service of the Word and the Lord's Supper, however, clearly constitute two distinct aspects of the assembly and each gave rise to special problems to which Paul now turns.

Paul's argument is extremely difficult to follow. The reason may be that he means to safeguard two distinct sets of values. The most fundamental values concern the equality and mutuality of men and women in the assembly. Both are one in the Lord, and both come from God (11:11–12). Such is the basis of their undifferentiated position vis-à-vis the community's prayers and prophetic activity.

However, given the community's tendency toward individualistic disintegration, he also finds it necessary to buttress a distinction in the matter of head covering (11:4–6), a distinction which parallels the accepted social practice according to which men wore their hair short while women wore it long (11:13–15). Arguing that women should wear a veil, Paul appeals to a distinction between men and women in the order of creation (11:7–10), a distinction which he immediately corrects with a statement on their equality (11:11–12).

Aware that his argument may not be too convincing and that the balance he tried to maintain between two sets of values is at best tenuous, he concludes the discussion by appealing to custom in the churches (11:16). Paul's purpose is thus to maintain a custom which should facilitate fidelity to the traditions which he had passed on to the Corinthians (11:2).

STUDY QUESTIONS: How is tradition related to Paul's principle of imitation? Why is Paul concerned about women wearing a veil in the assembly? Why does his position in this matter appear ambivalent?

17 Now that I am on the subject of instructions, I cannot say that you have done well in holding 18 meetings that do you more harm than good. ·In the first place, I hear that when you all come together as a community, there are separate factions 19 among you, and I half believe it—·since there must no doubt be separate groups among you, to dis- 20 tinguish those who are to be trusted. ·The point is, when you hold these meetings, it is not the 21 Lord's Supper that you are eating, ·since when the time comes to eat, everyone is in such a hurry to start his own supper that one person goes 22 hungry while another is getting drunk. ·Surely you have homes for eating and drinking in? Surely you have enough respect for the community of God not to make poor people embarrassed? What am I to say to you? Congratulate you? I cannot congratulate you on this.

23 For this is what I received from the Lord, and in turn passed on to you: that on the same night that he was betrayed, the Lord Jesus took some 24 bread, ·and thanked God for it and broke it, and he said, "This is my body, which is for you; do 25 this as a memorial of me." ·In the same way he took the cup after supper, and said, "This cup is the new covenant in my blood. Whenever you 26 drink it, do this as a memorial of me." ·Until the Lord comes, therefore, every time you eat this bread and drink this cup, you are proclaiming his 27 death, ·and so anyone who eats the bread or drinks the cup of the Lord unworthily will be behaving unworthily toward the body and blood of the Lord.

²⁸ Everyone is to recollect himself before eating
²⁹ this bread and drinking this cup; ·because a
person who eats and drinks without recognizing
the Body is eating and drinking his own con-
³⁰ demnation. ·In fact that is why many of you are
³¹ weak and ill and some of you have died. ·If only
we recollected ourselves, we should not be pun-
³² ished like that. ·But when the Lord does punish us
like that, it is to correct us and stop us from being
condemned with the world.

³³ So to sum up, my dear brothers, when you
³⁴ meet for the Meal, wait for one another. ·Anyone
who is hungry should eat at home, and then your
meeting will not bring your condemnation. The
other matters I shall adjust when I come.

✠

After dealing with a general problem concerning
order and decorum in the service of the Word (11:
2–16), Paul turns to very serious problems connected
with the celebration of the Lord's Supper (11:17–34).
These problems indicate a serious breakdown in the
community solidarity which lies at the very heart of the
Supper. In these matters, Paul finds no cause for commending the community (11:17,22b).

The problems now treated may not have been
brought up in the letter received from Corinth. If they
were, Paul does not allude to them as coming from this
source but rather as something concerning which he
has heard (11:18). It could also be, however, that the
letter had expressed these problems, but that Paul
views the divisions and factions in the assembly as a
specific manifestation of the factions reported to him
by members of Chloe's household (1:11). This last
view would explain both Paul's manner of introducing

the subject as well as its treatment among responses to
questions and affirmations made in the letter.

The unit includes a description of the problems
(11:18–22), a recall of the traditional liturgical formula used at the Lord's Supper (11:23–25), a brief reflection on the implications of this formula (11:26–27)
and an exhortation to act in a manner consistent with
the meaning of the eucharistic meal as it is spelled out
in the tradition (11:28–34).

First, Paul describes the general problem in terms of
divisions and factions within the assembly (1:18). The
factions actually allow someone to distinguish Christians who can be trusted from those who cannot be
trusted (1:19). Paul is against the divisions. However,
since the community includes both good and bad
members, they appear to be concretely unavoidable
and necessary. Addressing the community as a whole,
he attacks the social inequities and the lack of sharing
in the assembly. While the rich overindulge, the poor
go hungry. In such a context, one can hardly speak of
the Lord's Supper. Rather, each one is hurriedly eating
his own supper. There is consequently no point in the
community's gathering for the meal (11:20–22).

After this introductory description and response,
Paul cites the traditional liturgical formula which presents and interprets Jesus' action at the supper which
he shared on the night he was betrayed (11:23–27).
The liturgical text is thus intended as a norm of behavior in the community's celebration of the Lord's Supper. Christians must manifest the attitude of Jesus himself, a self-sacrificing attitude, and everything which is
inconsistent with this attitude must be excluded as con-
tradicting the nature of the meal. Jesus' meal expressed
the giving of his body for others and a new covenant
whose members were joined in his lifeblood. The his-

torical introduction which situated Jesus' supper on the night he was betrayed was a powerful message to a community which continued to betray the Lord by its factions and lack of sharing with the poor.

In 11:26, Paul develops the intrinsic meaning of the eucharistic memorial. The meal in which Christians express the attitude of Christ and give of themselves as he had given of himself is a proclamation of the Lord's death until his final coming. The Lord thus continues his historical action through the lives of Christians who express their commitment to others in the Christian meal. Unworthy participation, however, such as could be found at Corinth (11:17–22) constituted a betrayal of the community as well as of the body and blood of the Lord which each one was meant to proclaim (11:27).

In his exhortation, Paul points out that failure to give a true and honest expression to what the Eucharist is meant to be results in the condemnation of unworthy participants. In their failure to give life as Christ had given life, the Christians lose their own life. Their supper then becomes a countersign of the Lord's Supper, and it is counterproductive. They should consequently wait for one another and participate in a truly common meal (11:28–34).

STUDY QUESTIONS: What are the problems associated with the Corinthian community's eucharistic meal? How do these affect the celebration of the Lord's Supper? How does the quotation of a liturgical tradition serve Paul's argument? What is the fundamental significance of the eucharistic celebration?

1 Corinthians 12:1–30
UNITY AND DIVERSITY

1 **12** Now my dear brothers, I want to clear up a wrong impression about spiritual gifts.
2 You remember that, when you were pagans, whenever you felt irresistibly drawn, it was to-
3 ward dumb idols? ·It is for that reason that I want you to understand that on the one hand no one can be speaking under the influence of the Holy Spirit and say, "Curse Jesus," and on the other hand, no one can say, "Jesus is Lord," unless he is under the influence of the Holy Spirit.

4 There is a variety of gifts but always the same
5 Spirit; ·there are all sorts of service to be done,
6 but always to the same Lord; ·working in all sorts of different ways in different people, it is the
7 same God who is working in all of them. ·The particular way in which the Spirit is given to each
8 person is for a good purpose. ·One may have the gift of preaching with wisdom given him by the Spirit; another may have the gift of preaching
9 instruction given him by the same Spirit; ·and another the gift of faith given by the same Spirit; another again the gift of healing, through this one
10 Spirit; ·one, the power of miracles; another, prophecy; another the gift of recognizing spirits; another the gift of tongues and another the ability
11 to interpret them. ·All these are the work of one and the same Spirit, who distributes different gifts to different people just as he chooses.

12 Just as a human body, though it is made up of many parts, is a single unit because all these parts, though many, make one body, so it is with Christ.
13 In the one Spirit we were all baptized, Jews as

well as Greeks, slaves as well as citizens, and one
Spirit was given to us all to drink.

14 Nor is the body to be identified with any one of
15 its many parts. ·If the foot were to say, "I am not
a hand and so I do not belong to the body," would
that mean that it stopped being part of the body?
16 If the ear were to say, "I am not an eye, and so I
do not belong to the body," would that mean that
17 it was not a part of the body? ·If your whole body
was just one eye, how would you hear anything?
If it was just one ear, how would you smell anything?

18 Instead of that, God put all the separate parts
19 into the body on purpose. ·If all the parts were
20 the same, how could it be a body? ·As it is, the
21 parts are many but the body is one. ·The eye cannot say to the hand, "I do not need you," nor can
the head say to the feet, "I do not need you."

22 What is more, it is precisely the parts of the
body that seem to be the weakest which are the
23 indispensable ones; ·and it is the least honorable
parts of the body that we clothe with the greatest
care. So our more improper parts get decorated
24 in a way that our more proper parts do not need.
God has arranged the body so that more dignity
25 is given to the parts which are without it, ·and so
that there may not be disagreements inside the
body, but that each part may be equally con-
26 cerned for all the others. ·If one part is hurt, all
parts are hurt with it. If one part is given special
honor, all parts enjoy it.

27 Now you together are Christ's body; but each
28 of you is a different part of it. ·In the Church,
God has given the first place to apostles, the second to prophets, the third to teachers; after them,
miracles, and after them the gift of healing; help-
ers, good leaders, those with many languages.
29 Are all of them apostles, or all of them prophets,
or all of them teachers? Do they all have the gift
30 of miracles, ·or all have the gift of healing? Do
all speak strange languages, and all interpret
them?

✠

With 12:1, Paul takes up a fourth question (7:1, 25, 8:1) in the letter sent to him from Corinth. While the precise point of this question is unknown to us, it clearly had to do with spiritual gifts and their expression in the Christian assembly.

Paul finds it necessary to clear up a number of false impressions with regard to such gifts. There is no question that these are indeed manifestations of the Spirit. The latter's influence is absolutely fundamental to Christianity and to the most basic confession of faith in Jesus as Lord (12:2–3). The problem, however, resides in their diversity and in the conflicts which result from their manifestation in the community. Once again (11:2–16), Paul's attention focuses on the assembly's service of the word (12:1 – 14:40).

In his response, Paul emphasizes the role of the Holy Spirit (12:1–3) and the basic unity among the gifts of that Spirit, a unity revealed by their source in the one Spirit (12:4–11), their complementary contribution to the one body of Christ (12:12–30) and their relative position vis-à-vis Christian love, which transcends all the gifts (12:31 – 13:13). Such love orients the individual toward the common good, and the latter provides the criterion for distinguishing the relative importance (14:1–25) and for regulating the expression (14:26–40) of the various spiritual gifts in the assembly.

Gifts, services and works all refer to the same basic realities but from three different points of view. As manifestations of the energizing power of the same Spirit, those realities are termed gifts or charisms. As expressions of the ongoing mission of the one Lord, they are called services or ministries. From the point of view of their creative effects, they represent the works of one God. Gifts, services and works are thus distinguished and united in relation to the Trinity, and their multiplicity is seen in relation to one and the same Spirit, Lord or God (12:4–6). In 12:7–11, Paul lists a number of these gifts and insists on their common source in the same Spirit.

In 12:12–30, Paul addresses the question of diverse gifts directly and shows how concretely they are united not only in their source or origins (12:4–11) but in their coordination and purpose. To this end, he invokes the analogy of the human body, which illustrates how each part or member contributes to an organic whole or unit (12:12a,14–26). The body cannot be identified with any of its many parts, nor can any of the parts take the place of any other. Each contributes to the whole, which is dependent on the health and proper functioning of every one of its parts.

So it is with Christ (12:12b). In the one Spirit, distinctions between Jews and Greeks, slaves and citizens cease (12:13), but this does not obliterate differences in the ministerial gifts, some of which are more important than others but all of which are unique and essential to Christ's body, the Church (12:27–30).

STUDY QUESTIONS: How are gifts related to services (ministries) and to works? How are the various gifts related to one another?

1 Corinthians 12:31 – 13:13
THE PRIMACY OF LOVE

³¹ Be ambitious for the higher gifts. And I am going to show you a way that is better than any of them.

¹ **13** If I have all the eloquence of men or of angels, but speak without love, I am simply a gong booming or a cymbal clashing. ·If I have the gift of prophecy, understanding all the mysteries there are, and knowing everything, and if I have faith in all its fullness, to move mountains, but without love, then I am nothing at all. ³ If I give away all that I possess, piece by piece, and if I even let them take my body to burn it, but am without love, it will do me no good whatever.

⁴ Love is always patient and kind; it is never ⁵ jealous; love is never boastful or conceited; ·it is never rude or selfish; it does not take offense, ⁶ and is not resentful. ·Love takes no pleasure in ⁷ other people's sins but delights in the truth; ·it is always ready to excuse, to trust, to hope, and to endure whatever comes.

⁸ Love does not come to an end. But if there are gifts of prophecy, the time will come when they must fail; or the gift of languages, it will not continue for ever; and knowledge—for this, too, ⁹ the time will come when it must fail. ·For our knowledge is imperfect and our prophesying is ¹⁰ imperfect; ·but once perfection comes, all imperfect things will disappear. ·When I was a child, I used to talk like a child, and think like a child, and argue like a child, but now I am a ¹² man, all childish ways are put behind me. ·Now we are seeing a dim reflection in a mirror; but then we shall be seeing face to face. The knowl-

edge that I have now is imperfect; but then I
shall know as fully as I am known.

13   In short, there are three things that last: faith,
hope and love; and the greatest of these is love.

☩

In 12:1–30, Paul indicated the basis of Christian
unity for a community in which diversity of gifts has
become a source of conflict. In 12:31 – 13:13, he
shows how all the gifts are expressions of love, the one
reality which must be shared by all and which gives
meaning and value to all the gifts. The primacy of love
is thus presented as an important constitutive factor
which binds the diversely gifted members into one
community.

As Paul had shown in 12:28, there is a hierarchy
among the gifts. He now encourages the Corinthians to
seek after the higher gifts. Even as he does so, however, he insists on the way of love which transcends
them all (12:31). His statement proceeds in three
stages (13:1–3,4–8,9–12) and ends with a summary
(13:13).

The development begins with a conditional description of situations in which love is absent. Without love,
gifts of eloquence, prophecy, understanding and knowledge, extraordinary faith, the giving of one's goods and
even of one's life are of no value whatsoever (13:1–3).

Love is then related to other human and Christian
qualities, such as patience, kindness (13:4a), delight-
ing in the truth (13:7b), readiness to excuse, trust,
hope and endure (13:8). Between these positive statements, love is disassociated from rudeness, selfishness,
taking offense, resentfulness and taking pleasure in
other people's sins (13:5–7a).

The third section situates love and the gifts in relation to time and eternity (13:8–12). Only love is eternal. All the gifts will one day end (13:8), for they are imperfect and they will cease when perfection finally comes. At this point, Paul focuses on the community's preoccupation with knowledge or gnosis. Contrasting the present state, in which Christians see God as in a mirror, with their future face-to-face vision (13:12a), he finds an apt metaphor in the ways of a child which will eventually cede to mature adult ways (13:11). Like that of a child, present knowledge is imperfect. In their future face-to-face vision of God, their knowledge will reflect the divine knowledge itself. In eternity, knowledge will be mutual and we shall share in the perfection of God's own knowledge.

Summarizing, Paul refers to three Christian attitudes which are part and parcel of Christian life, faith, hope and love. The greatest of these is love (13:13), which does not end with this life (13:8a).

STUDY QUESTIONS: How is love related to the gifts? In terms of time and eternity, how is love related to faith?

1 Corinthians 14:1–25
PROPHECY AND THE GIFT OF TONGUES

¹ 14 You must want love more than anything else; but still hope for the spiritual gifts as ² well, especially prophecy. ·Anybody with the gift of tongues speaks to God, but not to other people; because nobody understands him when he ³ talks in the spirit about mysterious things. ·On the other hand, the man who prophesies does talk to other people, to their improvement, their en- ⁴ couragement and their consolation. ·The one with the gift of tongues talks for his own benefit, but the man who prophesies does so for the benefit ⁵ of the community. ·While I should like you all to have the gift of tongues, I would much rather you could prophesy, since the man who prophe- sies is of greater importance than the man with the gift of tongues, unless of course the latter of- fers an interpretation so that the church may get some benefit.

⁶ Now suppose, my dear brothers, I am someone with the gift of tongues, and I come to visit you, what use shall I be if all my talking reveals noth- ing new, tells you nothing, and neither inspires ⁷ you nor instructs you? ·Think of a musical in- strument, a flute or a harp: if one note on it cannot be distinguished from another, how can ⁸ you tell what tune is being played? ·Or if no one can be sure which call the trumpet has sounded, ⁹ who will be ready for the attack? ·It is the same with you: if your tongue does not produce intel- ligible speech, how can anyone know what you ¹⁰ are saying? You will be talking to the air. ·There are any number of different languages in the ¹¹ world, and not one of them is meaningless, ·but if

I am ignorant of what the sounds mean, I am a
savage to the man who is speaking, and he is a
12 savage to me. ·It is the same in your own case:
since you aspire to spiritual gifts, concentrate on
those which will grow to benefit the community.
13   That is why anybody who has the gift of
tongues must pray for the power of interpreting
14 them. ·For if I use this gift in my prayers, my
spirit may be praying but my mind is left barren.
15 What is the answer to that? Surely I should pray
not only with the spirit but with the mind as well?
And sing praises not only with the spirit but with
16 the mind as well? ·Any uninitiated person will
never be able to say Amen to your thanksgiving,
if you only bless God with the spirit, for he will
17 have no idea what you are saying. ·However well
you make your thanksgiving, the other gets no
18 benefit from it. ·I thank God that I have a greater
19 gift of tongues than all of you, ·but when I am in
the presence of the community I would rather say
five words that mean something than ten thousand
words in a tongue.
20   Brothers, you are not to be childish in your
outlook. You can be babies as far as wickedness
21 is concerned, but mentally you must be adult. ·In
the written Law it says: Through men speaking
strange languages and through the lips of foreign-
ers, I shall talk to the nation, and still they will
22 not listen to me, says the Lord. ·You see then,
that the strange languages are meant to be a sign
not for believers but for unbelievers, while on the
other hand, prophecy is a sign not for unbelievers
23 but for believers. ·So that any uninitiated people
or unbelievers, coming into a meeting of the
whole church where everybody was speaking in
24 tongues, would say you were all mad; ·but if you
were all prophesying and an unbeliever or uninitiated person came in, he would find himself
25 analyzed and judged by everyone speaking; ·he
would find his secret thoughts laid bare, and then
fall on his face and worship God, declaring that
God is among you indeed.

✠

After discussing the nature, unity (12:1–11) and complementarity (12:12–30) of gifts in the Christian community, as well as their relationship to Christian love (12:31 – 13:13), Paul turns to their relative importance (14:1–25). The passage is more concrete than the previous developments in this section (12:1 – 13:13). Referring to particular cases, the apostle emphasizes the criteria which should regulate attitudes toward the gifts as well as their expression in the assembly.

The unit is concerned with two gifts in particular, that of speaking in tongues and that of prophecy. It would appear that the community had been placing greater value on the gift of tongues. For Paul, this is problematic and another manifestation of rampant individualism in the assembly. Prophecy is actually a greater gift and one which meets community needs more adequately.

The gift of tongues is a good thing (14:5a,18). With it one speaks to God (14:2a). However, those who speak in tongues do so for their own benefit (14:4a) and not for that of the community, who cannot understand such talk. In community prayer, others must be able to understand the prayer in order to say Amen, and this presupposes that the members pray with their minds as well as with their spirit (14:14–19). This limitation can be offset by the power of interpretation (14:5c), and those who do speak in tongues must pray for this power (14:13).

The better to make his point, Paul evokes a hypothetical case in which he himself comes to the Corinthians speaking in tongues. He thus contrasts the behavior of those who insist on speaking in tongues with his own work of evangelization. Comparisons from music, the military call to battle, and the variety of human languages support his contention that orderly speech is essential. Human speech is not the same as mere sounds (14:6–12).

On the other hand, the gift of prophecy is on behalf of the community (14:3a), and this is of far greater value than the personal benefit which accrues from the gift of tongues (14:5b). Prophecy consists in the utterance of God's word for the improvement, encouragement and consolation of a community (14:3b). Of its very nature, it is meant to reveal something new or unperceived, to inspire and to instruct (14:6b). For Paul, the communal good which results from intelligible communication holds primacy over the private personal good (14:19). This position is directly related to the primacy of charity which Paul set forth in 12:31–13:13.

In the whole matter of prophecy and tongues, the Christians must be mature. They must not confuse the childlikeness, which is characteristic of virtuous living, with childishness in prayerful communication. Clinging to the gift of tongues is childish and immature (14:20).

Paul then develops the respective value of tongues and prophecy with regard to two categories which may be present in the assembly, those who are already believers and those who are interested in the faith but who are as yet unbelievers. It may be true that the gift of tongues benefits the unbelievers by demonstrating the divine presence, while prophecy is a sign for believers (14:22). Ultimately, however, even unbelievers will receive greater benefit from prophecy and its unveiling of the deeper self. The latter process leads directly to worship and the solid conviction of God's presence in the community (14:23–25).

STUDY QUESTIONS: What is meant by the gift of prophecy? How is the gift of tongues distinguished from the gift of prophecy? What are Paul's criteria for the public manifestation of the gift of tongues?

1 Corinthians 14:26–40
SEEKING THE COMMON GOOD

26 So, my dear brothers, what conclusion is to be drawn? At all your meetings, let everyone be ready with a psalm or a sermon or a revelation, or ready to use his gift of tongues or to give an interpretation; but it must always be for the

27 common good. ·If there are people present with the gift of tongues, let only two or three, at the most, be allowed to use it, and only one at a time,

28 and there must be someone to interpret. ·If there is no interpreter present, they must keep quiet in church and speak only to themselves and to God.

29 As for prophets, let two or three of them speak,

30 and the others attend to them. ·If one of the listeners receives a revelation, then the man who is

31 already speaking should stop. ·For you can all prophesy in turn, so that everybody will learn something and everybody will be encouraged.

32 Prophets can always control their prophetic

33 spirits, ·since God is not a God of disorder but of peace.

34 As in all the churches of the saints, ·women are to remain quiet at meetings since they have no permission to speak; they must keep in the

35 background as the Law itself lays it down. ·If they have any questions to ask, they should ask their husbands at home: it does not seem right for a woman to raise her voice at meetings.

36 Do you think the word of God came out of

37 yourselves? Or that it has come only to you? ·Anyone who claims to be a prophet or inspired ought to recognize that what I am writing to you is a

38 command from the Lord. ·Unless he recognizes this, you should not recognize him.

³⁹ And so, my dear brothers, by all means be ambitious to prophesy, do not suppress the gift of ⁴⁰ tongues, ·but let everything be done with propriety and in order.

☩

The long discussion of gifts (12:1 – 14:40) now concludes with a number of specific directives for good order in the assembly (14:26–40). The latter had been Paul's major preoccupation beginning with 11:2. Let all be ready to participate according to their gifts, but always with careful attention to the common good (14:26).

Concretely, this means that speaking in tongues must not dominate the assembly, that it must be done in orderly fashion, one at a time, and that only when an interpreter is present (14:27). Should there be no interpreter, speaking in tongues should be reserved for private prayer (14:28).

Prophecy must also be conducted in orderly fashion, in limited numbers and with one prophet speaking at a time. The others should listen carefully while the prophet speaks, but when a listener is gifted with a prophetic word, the prophet should pause and resume once the revelation has been shared (14:29–31). The very nature of prophecy includes and calls for such control (14:32). It is God who speaks through the prophet (14:36–38), and God is not the source of disorder (14:33).

Pursuing his discussion of the role and conduct of women in the assembly (11:2–16), Paul then asks that they remain silent. For this he appeals to common practice in all the churches (14:34) and to the Law (14:35a). There are thus circumstances where the

Law remains in effect, or at least where Paul does
not hesitate to appeal to it. Immediate pastoral concerns are more important to Paul than theological
consistency. This final directive is more stringent
than what Paul recognizes and allows in 11:5, which
dealt with womanly decorum while praying and prophesying in public worship. This development seems to
have been occasioned by the overriding need for order
and the common good. After discussing the gifts, Paul
has become even more sensitive to these than he had
been in the earlier part of the letter. His directive, however, is relative to the difficult situation at Corinth and
must not be taken as an absolute statement for all
times. Indicating that women should consult their husbands concerning questions which had arisen once they
returned home, Paul registers a certain hesitation and
points out that questioning by women in the assembly
appears to be unseemly (14:35b).

Ultimately all must recognize that the word of God
is from God and not from the Christians themselves.
To prophesy or not to prophesy is consequently not a
matter of personal right or choice (14:36–38). Indeed
the Christians may hope for the gift of prophecy, and
they should. By the same token, they should not suppress tongues which are also of God (14:29). However, propriety and order must remain paramount
(14:30).

STUDY QUESTIONS: How does the situation at Corinth
affect Paul's views concerning
women speaking in the assembly?
How does the divine source of
prophecy contribute to Paul's argument for order?

1 Corinthians 15:1–11
THE RESURRECTION OF CHRIST

¹ 15 Brothers, I want to remind you of the gospel I preached to you, the gospel that you received and in which you are firmly estab- ² lished; ·because the gospel will save you only if you keep believing exactly what I preached to you—believing anything else will not lead to anything.

³ Well then, in the first place, I taught you what I had been taught myself, namely that Christ died for our sins, in accordance with the scriptures; ⁴ that he was buried; and that he was raised to life on the third day, in accordance with the scrip- ⁵ tures; ·that he appeared first to Cephas and sec- ⁶ ondly to the Twelve. ·Next he appeared to more than five hundred of the brothers at the same time, most of whom are still alive, though some ⁷ have died; ·then he appeared to James, and then ⁸ to all the apostles; ·and last of all he appeared to me too; it was as though I was born when no one expected it.

⁹ I am the least of the apostles; in fact, since I persecuted the Church of God, I hardly deserve ¹⁰ the name apostle; ·but by God's grace that is what I am, and the grace that he gave me has not been fruitless. On the contrary, I, or rather the grace of God that is with me, have worked harder ¹¹ than any of the others; ·but what matters is that I preach what they preach, and this is what you all believed.

✠

Having responded to the question concerning the gifts of the Spirit (12:1 – 14:40), Paul takes up the matter of the resurrection of the dead (15:1–58). He does not appear to have been questioned in this matter, but he is aware that some are denying the resurrection of the dead (15:12). In his response, Paul shows how this denial, which refers to the resurrection of Christians, is inconsistent with faith in the resurrection of Christ.

The denial of the resurrection underlies the many problems at Corinth, for it provided special justification for the libertine attitudes which developed in a segment of the community (15:33–34) alongside exaggerated asceticism. It should be noted that the same attitudes could have arisen from belief that the kingdom had already arrived and in effect that the resurrection was already realized. For Paul, however, this view would have been tantamount to a denial of the resurrection. The risen state is quite other than the present historical state of Christians.

The chapter can be divided into four units. First, Paul presents an early Christian creed and its place in the faith of the Corinthians as well as in his own apostolic work (15:1–11). Second, he shows how denial of the resurrection is incompatible with the Corinthians' faith in the resurrection of Christ (15:12–34). Third, he responds to what might be the basis of non-belief among the Corinthians, namely, a false idea about the nature of the resurrection (15:35–53). Fourth and finally, he sings in thanksgiving for God's extraordinary gift of resurrection and concludes with a brief exhortation (15:54–58).

In 15:1–3a, Paul introduces the subject by recalling the Gospel creed which he had preached at Corinth, which he himself had received, which the Corinthians had accepted and on which their faith was firmly established. The traditional creed is brief, but every term is significant. The death of Christ is not meaningless but purposeful and to be understood according to the scriptures. His burial evokes the baptismal context of those who accepted to be buried with Christ. His resurrection is "on the third day," an expression which evokes God's universal salvation, and it too is to be understood according to the scriptures. Finally, the appearances of the risen Christ to Cephas and to the Twelve, who were associated with Antioch, is an experience of God's glory (15:3b–5).

Paul then supplements the creed by noting appearances to five hundred at once, to James and the apostles, figures associated with Jerusalem, and to himself (15:6–8a). Unlikely as this last appearance might seem, it was undeniable and allowed Paul to profess his faith in continuity with those who first came to know the risen Lord (15:8b).

This first section ends with further personal considerations, which contrast Paul's previous life as a persecutor with the way grace has elevated him among the apostles (15:9–10), and which reaffirm the opening statements of 15:1–3a. There is no distinction between Paul's preaching and that of the other apostles; nor is there any difference between the belief of the Corinthian Christians and the traditional preaching they had received (15:11).

STUDY QUESTIONS: How does one's view concerning the resurrection condition Christian behavior and attitudes? What are the elements of the early Christian creed which Paul cites in 1 Co 15:3b–5? Why was it important to mention the appearance to Paul?

1 Corinthians 15:12–34
THE RESURRECTION OF CHRISTIANS

¹² Now if Christ raised from the dead is what has been preached, how can some of you be saying ¹³ that there is no resurrection of the dead? ·If there is no resurrection of the dead, Christ him- ¹⁴ self cannot have been raised, ·and if Christ has not been raised then our preaching is useless and ¹⁵ your believing it is useless; ·indeed, we are shown up as witnesses who have committed perjury be- fore God, because we swore in evidence before ¹⁶ God that he raised Christ to life. ·For if the dead ¹⁷ are not raised, Christ has not been raised, ·and if Christ has not been raised, you are still in your ¹⁸ sins. ·And what is more serious, all who have died ¹⁹ in Christ have perished. ·If our hope in Christ has been for this life only, we are the most unfor- tunate of all people.

²⁰ But Christ has in fact been raised from the dead, the first fruits of all who have fallen asleep. ²¹ Death came through one man and in the same way the resurrection of the dead has come ²² through one man. ·Just as all men die in Adam, ²³ so all men will be brought to life in Christ; ·but all of them in their proper order: Christ as the first fruits and then, after the coming of Christ, ²⁴ those who belong to him. ·After that will come the end, when he hands over the kingdom to God the Father, having done away with every sov- ²⁵ ereignty, authority and power. ·For he must be king until he has put all his enemies under his ²⁶ feet ·and the last of the enemies to be destroyed is death, for everything is to be put under his feet. ²⁷ —Though when it is said that everything is sub- jected, this clearly cannot include the One who

28 subjected everything to him. ·And when everything is subjected to him, then the Son himself will be subject in his turn to the One who subjected all things to him, so that God may be all in all.

29 If this were not true, what do people hope to gain by being baptized for the dead? If the dead are not ever going to be raised, why be baptized

30 on their behalf? ·What about ourselves? Why are

31 we living under a constant threat? ·I face death every day, brothers, and I can swear it by the pride that I take in you in Christ Jesus our Lord.

32 If my motives were only human ones, what good would it do me to fight the wild animals at

33 Ephesus? ·You say: Let us eat and drink today; tomorrow we shall be dead. You must stop being led astray: "Bad friends ruin the noblest people."

34 Come to your senses, behave properly, and leave sin alone; there are some of you who seem not to know God at all; you should be ashamed.

✠

Denial of the resurrection is altogether incompatible with faith in the resurrection of Christ. Such is Paul's basic point in 15:12-34. After arguing it (15:12-19), the apostle provides a brief synopsis of belief in the resurrection of Christ and of Christians (15:20-28), and he shows the absurdity of the contrary position in terms of Christian life, practice and commitment (15:29-34). Throughout the passage, he presupposes that the Corinthians actually do believe that Jesus is risen. Apart from such faith, Paul's argument would not stand.

The contradiction in the position of some Corinthians lies in their grounds for denying the resurrection of Christians. By denying the resurrection of the dead in itself and as an absolute impossibility, they mean to take a stand on the resurrection of Christians, but in actual fact their denial also implies a rejection of Christ's resurrection. Stated absolutely, their position allows for no exceptions. In this, however, they are inconsistent, for they do in fact believe that Christ is risen (15:1–5). Consequently, their basis for denying the resurrection of Christians is invalid. Rhetorically, Paul then takes up the consequences of their position. Not only would his preaching be in vain, but they would remain in their sins, those who have died would have perished, and Christian hope would be groundless (15:12–19).

Paul then turns to a positive elaboration of Christian faith in the matter. Christ has indeed been raised from the dead. This, however, was not an isolated event. Risen, he is the first fruits of God's Christian harvest. This is due to the very nature of the resurrection event, which established Christ as the first man of a new creation. Christ's role in human history thus corresponds to that of Adam. In Adam we die; in Christ we live, but according to a certain order. After Christ's resurrection will come that of all who are his. At that moment, which heralds the end, the kingdom will be fulfilled and presented to God. All contrary powers will then be destroyed. God's sovereignty will be absolute and reflected in all of creation (15:20–28). In his exposition, Paul provides a marvelous statement concerning the nature, development and fulfillment of the kingdom of God.

With 15:29, the apostle resumes his effort to spell out the consequences of the Corinthian denial of the resurrection (see 15:14–19). Since Christ's salvific work extends to both the living and the dead

(15:20–28), so do the Christian efforts of those who extend and express that work in history.

In baptism, Christians die with Christ that others might live and their sacramental death is on behalf of both the living and the dead. Such a baptism, however, would be meaningless if the dead were not to benefit and be raised to life (15:29). The same is true of the risks which Christians take in fulfilling their baptismal commitment (15:30–32). The unit concludes with a sharply worded exhortation to behave according to one's Christian nature and to put aside all self-serving efforts to justify a life of sin. These are not in keeping with belief in the resurrection (15:33–34).

STUDY QUESTIONS: In light of 1 Co 15:20–28, what is the meaning of the petition "Thy kingdom come" in the Lord's prayer? How is baptism related to belief in the resurrection of Christians?

1 Corinthians 15:35–58
THE NATURE OF THE RESURRECTION

35 Someone may ask, "How are dead people raised, and what sort of body do they have when
36 they come back?" ·They are stupid questions. Whatever you sow in the ground has to die before
37 it is given new life ·and the thing that you sow is not what is going to come; you sow a bare grain,
38 say of wheat or something like that, ·and then God gives it the sort of body that he has chosen: each sort of seed gets its own sort of body.
39 Everything that is flesh is not the same flesh: there is human flesh, animals' flesh, the flesh of
40 birds and the flesh of fish. ·Then there are heavenly bodies and there are earthly bodies; but the heavenly bodies have a beauty of their own and
41 the earthly bodies a different one. ·The sun has its brightness, the moon a different brightness, and the stars a different brightness, and the stars
42 differ from each other in brightness. ·It is the same with the resurrection of the dead: the thing that is sown is perishable but what is raised is im-
43 perishable; ·the thing that is sown is contemptible but what is raised is glorious; the thing that is
44 sown is weak but what is raised is powerful; ·when it is sown it embodies the soul, when it is raised it embodies the spirit.

If the soul has its own embodiment, so does the
45 spirit have its own embodiment. ·The first man, Adam, as scripture says, became a living soul; but the last Adam has become a life-giving spirit.
46 That is, first the one with the soul, not the spirit,
47 and after that, the one with the spirit. ·The first man, being from the earth, is earthly by nature;
48 the second man is from heaven. ·As this earthly

man was, so are we on earth; and as the heav-
⁴⁹ enly man is, so are we in heaven. ·And we, who
have been modeled on the earthly man, will be
modeled on the heavenly man.

⁵⁰   Or else, brothers, put it this way: flesh and
blood cannot inherit the kingdom of God: and
the perishable cannot inherit what lasts for ever.
⁵¹ I will tell you something that has been secret: that
we are not all going to die, but we shall all be
⁵² changed. ·This will be instantaneous, in the
twinkling of an eye, when the last trumpet sounds.
It will sound, and the dead will be raised, im-
⁵³ perishable, and we shall be changed as well, ·be-
cause our present perishable nature must put on
imperishability and this mortal nature must put
on immortality.

⁵⁴   When this perishable nature has put on imperishability, and when this mortal nature has
put on immortality, then the words of scripture
will come true: Death is swallowed up in victory.
⁵⁵ Death, where is your victory? Death, where is
⁵⁶ your sting? ·Now the sting of death is sin, and sin
⁵⁷ gets its power from the Law. ·So let us thank God
for giving us the victory through our Lord Jesus
Christ.

⁵⁸   Never give in then, my dear brothers, never
admit defeat; keep on working at the Lord's
work always, knowing that, in the Lord, you
cannot be laboring in vain.

✠

In Paul's judgment, the Corinthians have based their
denial of the resurrection on a false conception of its
nature. In their understanding or imagination, they saw
it as a return to the perishable life which had ceased at
death. For people who distinguished between body and
soul and who believed that the soul was liberated from
its bodily shackles at death, the resurrection appeared

senseless. Paul responds by affirming the continuity and the discontinuity between the earthly life of those who die and the heavenly life of those who rise (15:35–53).

The Pauline response begins with an image from agriculture. Surely there is continuity between the seed that is sown and dies and the new life which springs from it. At the same time, the identical seed does not emerge from the ground but a new plant with a unique life or "body" of its own (15:35–38). He then lists different kinds of flesh and bodies and insists on the beauty characteristic of each. All are not reducible to the same kind of body (15:39–41). He then applies the foregoing to the resurrection. The body of the risen is imperishable, glorious and filled with the Spirit. It differs from our earthly bodies, which are perishable, contemptible and filled with the soul (15:42–44a).

The primary principles of human life are the soul and the Spirit, and each has its own embodiment. Pursuing the scriptural relationship of Christ to Adam (15:21–22), Paul distinguishes the life-giving Spirit of Christ from the living soul of Adam. While the former is heavenly, the latter is earthly. They thus provide the model for understanding the heavenly life of those who will be raised from the dead and the earthly life of those who continue to live in history (15:44b–49).

Paul then affirms the necessity of our transformation. Flesh and blood cannot inherit a kingdom which is everlasting. For this, one needs to be filled with the imperishable Spirit. Accordingly, when the end comes, even the living will abandon their perishable and mortal nature and receive imperishability and immortality (15:50–53).

The entire chapter on the resurrection (15:1–58) concludes with a quasi-hymnic exclamation of wonder and thanksgiving over life's ultimate victory over death, which God has rendered harmless and impotent (15:54–57). In this final statement, Paul exhorts the Corinthians to persevere in the Lord's work. They are not laboring in vain (15:58). In positive tones, he thus sweeps away all hypothetical suggestions that Christian belief (15:2), preaching (15:14), life (15:17–18), hope (15:19), practice (15:29), persecutions and sufferings (15:30–32) are in vain.

STUDY QUESTIONS: What are the implications of Paul's image of the seed with regard to the nature of the resurrection? How is the Spirit related to the resurrection?

1 Corinthians 16:1–24
FINAL QUESTIONS AND GREETING

¹ **16** Now about the collection made for the saints: you are to do as I told the churches ² in Galatia to do. ·Every Sunday, each one of you must put aside what he can afford, so that collec- ³ tions need not be made after I have come. ·When I am with you, I will send your offering to Jeru- salem by the hand of whatever men you give ⁴ letters of reference to; ·if it seems worth while for me to go too, they can travel with me.

⁵ I shall be coming to you after I have passed through Macedonia—and I am doing no more ⁶ than pass through Macedonia—·and I may be staying with you, perhaps even passing the win- ter, to make sure that it is you who send me on ⁷ my way wherever my travels take me. ·As you see, I do not want to make it only a passing visit to you and I hope to spend some time with you, ⁸ the Lord permitting. ·In any case I shall be stay- ⁹ ing at Ephesus until Pentecost ·because a big and important door has opened for my work and there is a great deal of opposition.

¹⁰ If Timothy comes, show him that he has noth- ing to be afraid of in you: like me, he is doing the ¹¹ Lord's work, ·and nobody is to be scornful of him. Send him happily on his way to come back to me; the brothers and I are waiting for him.

¹² As for our brother Apollos, I begged him to come to you with the brothers but he was quite firm that he did not want to go yet and he will come as soon as he can.

¹³ Be awake to all the dangers; stay firm in the ¹⁴ faith; be brave and be strong. ·Let everything you do be done in love.

¹⁵ There is something else to ask you, brothers.

You know how the Stephanas family, who were
the first fruits of Achaia, have really worked hard
16 to help the saints. ·Well, I want you in your turn
to put yourselves at the service of people like this,
17 and anyone who helps and works with them. ·I
am delighted that Stephanas, Fortunatus and
Achaicus have arrived; they make up for your
18 absence. ·They have settled my mind, and yours
too; I hope you appreciate men like this.
19   All the churches of Asia send you greetings.
Aquila and Prisca, with the church that meets at
their house, send you their warmest wishes, in
20 the Lord. ·All the brothers send you their greetings. Greet one another with a holy kiss.
21   This greeting is in my own hand—Paul.
22   If anyone does not love the Lord, a curse on
him. "Maran atha."
23   The grace of the Lord Jesus be with you.
24   My love is with you all in Christ Jesus.

✠

The letter to the Corinthians has now come to its
conclusion. Responding to a final question (7:1,25,
8:1, 12:1), Paul provides directives concerning the
collection on behalf of poor Christians (16:1-4). This
collection is an important indication of the growing
sense of solidarity among the churches and one of the
historical stepping-stones in the emergence of the universal Church. Contextually, it is intimately related to
Paul's own travels and his intention to personally return to Corinth after Pentecost (16:4–8). In the meantime, he intends to remain in Ephesus where opposition has not prevented opportunity for evangelization
(16:9).

The letter thus ends by recalling Paul's projected
visit (4:18–21), which more recent events have
delayed for a time. It also reminds the Corinthians of

Timothy's coming (4:17, 16:10–11) and once again
brings up the subject of Apollos (1:10–4:21), who is
now with Paul. The apostle's positive attitude toward
Apollos is clear. Paul had begged Apollos to return to
Corinth, but the latter was adamant in delaying his trip
to that city (16:12).

A brief and general moral exhortation (16:13–14)
is followed by a request that the Corinthians recognize
and aid the leadership of Stephanas and his family
(1:16, 16:15–16). These first Achaian Christians had
stood firm through difficulties. Stephanas himself, together with Fortunatus and Achaicus were now with
Paul (16:17) where they represented the whole
Corinthian church. Upon their return, they should be
well-received and appreciated (16:18). Just as they
had borne the letter from Corinth, they would now
bear Paul's letter to Corinth and represent him in the
community.

With Paul's letter go greetings from the church of
Asia, and especially from Aquila and Prisca and the
church which assembles in their house. Aquila and
Prisca were well known to the Corinthians (Acts
18:1–3). They had accompanied Paul as far as
Ephesus after his long stay in Corinth (Acts
18:18–19) and had been instrumental in supple-
menting the instruction of Apollos (Acts 18:24–26).
The concluding blessings and wishes are both liturgically inspired and highly personal (16:20,22–24),
written not in the hand of the secretary but of Paul
himself (16:21; see 2 Th 3:17, Ga 6:11).

STUDY QUESTIONS: How is the collection on behalf of
poor Christians related to the uni-
versality of the Church? What was
the role of Stephanas in Paul's
communication with Corinth?

2 Corinthians
The Second Letter of Paul
to the Church at Corinth

INTRODUCTION

The first letter to the church at Corinth may have resolved some problems but it also appears to have aggravated others. When Paul failed to arrive in Corinth as he had announced, those who opposed him in the community accused him of dishonesty, inconsistency and of having written to them as he did merely to curry favor with them. Paul's word was little more than a vain boast! A visit from Timothy and even a brief, hurried visit from Paul himself had done little or nothing to ameliorate the situation.

When news of these negative reactions reached Paul, it compounded the difficulties which surrounded his work at Ephesus. Deeply involved in the evangelization of that city, he immediately sent Titus to Corinth in his place. His mission was to resolve the problems, present Paul's position and effect a reconciliation. Paul's plan was that the two should meet later at Troas. However, when Paul finally went to that city, Titus had not yet returned, and so he moved on to Macedonia, where further troubles awaited him. Finally, Titus did arrive. The news was good. His mission was a success. It is at this time that Paul wrote the second letter to the church at Corinth. The sequence of events bears some similarity to that which led to the writing of 1 Thessalonians.

Attacked in his very apostolic mission and the way he was exercising it, Paul responded by defending his actions and motives. In so doing he presented an extraordinary and highly developed statement of his

apostolic ministry and its significance. It is found in the
first and third parts of the letter (1:12–7:16,
10:1–13:10). The second part of the letter treats of
the collection for the poor (8:1–9:15) which Paul
had requested in his first letter. The good news brought
by Titus had not dispelled Paul's need to respond to
the earlier problems. In actual fact he was not so sure
that all of these had been eliminated.

Difficulties and conflicts in the exercising of church
leadership did not die with Paul. Neither did the need
for contributing to the support of churches afflicted by
poverty. We are thus invited to enter the Corinthian
situation through which we can then assess the scope
and nature of our problems. We are also invited to join
Paul in his response to those problems as he draws on
his letter writer's skill to form and orient the community in a positive direction. Paul's astuteness can be
measured by the way he promoted the collection for
the poor, even as he struggled to establish his credentials and honesty as an apostle. Few have faced so
great a challenge.

2 Corinthians 1:1–11
ADDRESS AND THANKSGIVING

¹ From Paul, appointed by God to be an apostle of Christ Jesus, and from Timothy, one of the brothers, to the church of God at Corinth and to ² all the saints in the whole of Achaia. ·Grace and peace to you from God our Father and the Lord Jesus Christ.

³ Blessed be the God and Father of our Lord Jesus Christ, a gentle Father and the God of all ⁴ consolation, ·who comforts us in all our sorrows, so that we can offer others, in their sorrows, the consolation that we have received from God our- ⁵ selves. ·Indeed, as the sufferings of Christ over- flow to us, so, through Christ, does our consola- ⁶ tion overflow. ·When we are made to suffer, it is for your consolation and salvation. When, in- stead, we are comforted, this should be a con- solation to you, supporting you in patiently bear- ⁷ ing the same sufferings as we bear. ·And our hope for you is confident, since we know that, sharing our sufferings, you will also share our conso- lations.

⁸ For we should like you to realize, brothers, that the things we had to undergo in Asia were more of a burden than we could carry, so that we de- ⁹ spaired of coming through alive. ·Yes, we were carrying our own death warrant with us, and it has taught us not to rely on ourselves but only on ¹⁰ God, who raises the dead to life. ·And he saved us from dying, as he will save us again; yes, that is our firm hope in him, that in the future he will ¹¹ save us again. ·You must all join in the prayers for us; the more people there are asking for help for

us, the more will be giving thanks when it is
granted to us.

✠

2 Corinthians opens with a specifically Christian
form of address and greeting (1:1–2), recognizable
from Paul's previous letters. As in 1 Co 1:1, Paul's insistence on the divine source of his apostleship responds to the Corinthian challenge, where many questioned Paul's apostolic credentials. As we shall see, the
defense of Paul's apostleship, and of his manner of exercising it, constitutes one of the letter's fundamental
preoccupations.

Like 1 and 2 Thessalonians and 1 Corinthians, the
letter has a co-sender. He is Timothy, one of the
brothers who had accompanied Paul in the first mission
to Macedonia, who had joined Paul and Silvanus at
Corinth and who had been a co-sender of the two letters to the church at Thessalonika. Later, during the
Ephesian mission, Paul had sent Timothy back to
Corinth (1 Co 4:17, 16:10–12), and he had been
away during the writing of 1 Corinthians. However, he
had since rejoined Paul in Macedonia with news of developments at Corinth and in particular of how Paul's
earlier letter had been received by the Christians of
that city.

Unlike the first letter, which was addressed to the
Corinthians and to others in general, the present letter
is to the church at Corinth and to all Christians in the
province of Achaia, of which Corinth was the Roman
capital. Paul's work of evangelization is thus focused
on the administrative, political and commercial center.

Through that center, however, he directs the Gospel to the entire region.

Whereas, in most of his other letters, Paul's thanksgiving unit consists in a report concerning his prayer, 2 Co 1:3–11 includes an actual prayer of blessing. God is blessed as a gentle Father and the God of all consolations, as a comforter who enables Paul to extend to others the consolation he has received (1:3–4). With this prayer, Paul introduces the tone of the entire letter. Paul has suffered. However, others also have suffered. Paul recognizes his responsibility in this regard and reaches out to them with the consolation of Christ.

Paul's sufferings represent the overflow of Christ's sufferings, and like the sufferings of Christ they are salvific. Through Christ, the consolation which followed Paul's sufferings also overflows onto others and should support them in their own sufferings (1:5–6). Paul is now at peace and his apostolic hope is secure. Those who share in his sufferings will also share in his consolations (1:7).

The sufferings to which Paul refers came at the hands of certain people in Asia who Paul evangelized from Ephesus, the capital of the Roman province (1:8). Paul had already referred to opposition in that city while outlining his future plans at the end of his first letter to Corinth (1 Co 16:9). The opposition, however, had turned out to be far more severe and aggressive than Paul had then estimated. With his life threatened and death an ever-present possibility, he had not desisted from the mission. Taught to rely on God alone, he had been saved, and the God who raises the dead to life would save him again in the future. The death and resurrection of Jesus thus provided him with the pattern for understanding Christian suffering and salvation (1:8–11). These troubles in Asia had later been compounded by further difficulties in Macedonia (7:5).

Paul's sufferings had not come from Asians and Macedonians alone. Continuing troubles, accusations and resistance to his letter at Corinth had also contributed. Writing to the Corinthians, he wants them to be aware that they had added to his troubles. However, since many of them had shared in his sufferings, they would also share in his consolations (1:7).

STUDY QUESTIONS: What are the elements in Paul's prayer of blessing (1:3–4)? How does Paul view the meaning of Christian suffering?

REASONS FOR DELAYING HIS VISIT

12 There is one thing we are proud of, and our conscience tells us it is true: that we have always treated everybody, and especially you, with the reverence and sincerity which come from God, and by the grace of God we have done this with-
13 out ulterior motives. ·There are no hidden meanings in our letters besides what you can read for
14 yourselves and understand. ·And I hope that, although you do not know us very well yet, you will have come to recognize, when the day of our Lord Jesus comes, that you can be as proud of us as we are of you.

15 Because I was so sure of this, I had meant to come to you first, so that you would benefit
16 doubly; ·staying with you before going to Macedonia and coming back to you again on the way back from Macedonia, for you to see me on my
17 way to Judaea. ·Do you think I was not sure of my own intentions when I planned this? Do you really think that when I am making my plans, my motives are ordinary human ones, and that I
18 say Yes, yes, and No, no, at the same time? ·I swear by God's truth, there is no Yes and No
19 about what we say to you. ·The Son of God, the Christ Jesus that we proclaimed among you—I mean Silvanus and Timothy and I—was never Yes
20 and No: with him it was always Yes, ·and however many the promises God made, the Yes to them all is in him. That is why it is "through him"
21 that we answer Amen to the praise of God. ·Remember it is God himself who assures us all, and you, of our standing in Christ, and has anointed

22 us, ·marking us with his seal and giving us the pledge, the Spirit, that we carry in our hearts.

23 By my life, I call God to witness that the reason why I did not come to Corinth after all was to
24 spare your feelings. ·We are not dictators over your faith, but are fellow workers with you for your happiness; in the faith you are steady
1 enough. 2 Well then, I made up my mind not to
2 pay you a second distressing visit. ·I may have hurt you, but if so I have hurt the only people
3 who could give me any pleasure. ·I wrote as I did to make sure that, when I came, I should not be distressed by the very people who should have made me happy. I am sure you all know that I
4 could never be happy unless you were. ·When I wrote to you, in deep distress and anguish of mind, and in tears, it was not to make you feel hurt but to let you know how much love I have for you.

5 Someone has been the cause of pain; and the cause of pain not to me, but to some degree—not
6 to overstate it—to all of you. ·The punishment already imposed by the majority on the man in
7 question is enough; ·and the best thing now is to give him your forgiveness and encouragement, or
8 he might break down from so much misery. ·So I am asking you to give some definite proof of
9 your love for him. ·What I really wrote for, after all, was to test you and see whether you are com-
10 pletely obedient. ·Anybody that you forgive, I forgive; and as for my forgiving anything—if there has been anything to be forgiven, I have forgiven it for your sake in the presence of
11 Christ. ·And so we will not be outwitted by Satan —we know well enough what his intentions are.

✠

The first part of 2 Corinthians includes reflections on why Paul changed his plans to visit Corinth in the near future (1:12 – 2:11) and a long discussion on the nature and concrete implications of Paul's apostolic ministry (2:12 – 7:16). The entire section is framed by considerations concerning the reaction to the letter which Paul had earlier written to Corinth (1:12 – 2:11, 7:5–16).

In 1 Co 4:18–21, Paul had announced that he would soon come to Corinth. In the meantime he had sent Timothy (1 Co 4:17) and 1 Corinthians, the oldest extant letter which he had written to them. In 1 Co 16:2–3, he had again referred to his coming visit, which would take place after Pentecost (1 Co 16:8), following a visit to Macedonia (1 Co 16:5). He had gone so far as to announce that he would remain at Corinth for an extended period, perhaps even the entire winter (1 Co 16:6). However, when Timothy returned to Ephesus with news that all was not well in Corinth (7:8–9), Paul seems to have made a hurried visit to the community and quickly returned to his work at Ephesus (2:1). This extra visit, however, had not fulfilled his original intention to spend a fairly long period at Corinth, and he had yet to fulfill that promise.

Paul's plans had subsequently evolved to include two visits, one before going to Macedonia and one on his return (2 Co 1:15–16). Whence he had intended to go on to Judaea (2 Co 1:16) and Jerusalem with the collection for the relief of Christians in those parts (1 Co 16:1–4). That collection is the subject of the second part of this letter (2 Co 8:1 – 9:15).

Paul's plans, however, had been even further revised. Months had passed, and he had not yet gone to Corinth. A second emissary, Titus (12:16–18), had taken a long time to return (2:13). In light of the reception granted to Paul's first letter, of Timothy's visit, and of Paul's own hurried visit, which does not appear to have been a pleasant one, Titus' delay was not reassuring. It may have been the immediate and concrete occasion for putting off the visit to Corinth and for the longer sojourn in Macedonia (2:13).

Many Corinthians, however, had been eagerly awaiting Paul's visit, and when he failed to arrive, some unfriendly voices once again rose in accusation: Paul was proud (1:12), his word was not to be trusted (1:17), and his letters were full of hidden meanings (1:13).

In his response, Paul attests to the sincerity and straightforwardness of his motives (1:12–13). One day these should become obvious (1:14). Paul had truly intended to visit them as he said, and his word had been spoken in the truth of God who anointed him for his Christian mission with the Spirit of truth (1:15–22). Given the troubled situation at Corinth, however, he had decided not to come immediately. His visit would have been a painful and distressing one for him as well as for them, and in his judgment the pastoral situation did not require this (1:23–2:4).

In setting out his motives, Paul refers to his projected visit as "a second distressing visit" (2:1). There had thus been a first, and the second refers to Paul's hurried visit after Timothy's return to Ephesus. This accords well with Paul's announced plans for a third trip to Corinth in 12:14 and 13:1.

Given the difficulties which continued to plague the community and the painful history of Paul's relationship to it, the letter written "in deep distress and anguish of mind, and in tears" (2:4) very likely refers not to 1 Corinthians but to a subsequent letter. This additional letter would fit the circumstances surrounding Paul's "second distressing visit" (2:1). We would thus know of four letters written to Corinth: that referred to in 1 Co 5:9–13, that which is now 1 Corinthians, the letter described in 2 Co 2:4, and the present 2 Corinthians. Be that as it may, at first Paul's letter had not had the desired effect, which was to relieve the distressing situation.

In 1:12–2:4, Paul discusses the first reaction to his letter. As he affirms, however, Titus had later been able to assure him that the Corinthians had since had a change of heart (7:6–7,13–16). Paul's letter had finally had its intended effect, and he has no regrets (7:8).

In 2:5–11, Paul refers to someone who had caused pain to both himself and the community at Corinth. The person in question could be any of several with whose case Paul had dealt in 1 Corinthians or in the letter which followed his second visit. Paul had obviously taken a harsher line of conduct than that which the Corinthians actually followed. He now joins the community in forgiving the repentant person. The data given in 2:5–11 corresponds fairly well to the situation and Pauline response indicated in 1 Co 5:1–8.

STUDY QUESTIONS: How did changes in Paul's travel plans affect the Corinthian community? What factors led him to change his plans? What indications do we have that not all of Paul's letters came to be included in the New Testament?

MINISTERS OF A NEW COVENANT

¹² When I went up to Troas to preach the Good News of Christ, and the door was wide open for ¹³ my work there in the Lord, ·I was so continually uneasy in mind at not meeting brother Titus there, I said good-by to them and went on to Macedonia.

¹⁴ Thanks be to God who, wherever he goes, makes us, in Christ, partners of his triumph, and through us is spreading the knowledge of him- ¹⁵ self, like a sweet smell, everywhere. ·We are Christ's incense to God for those who are being ¹⁶ saved and for those who are not; ·for the last, the smell of death that leads to death, for the first the sweet smell of life that leads to life. And who ¹⁷ could be qualified for work like this? ·At least we do not go around offering the word of God for sale, as many other people do. In Christ, we speak as men of sincerity, as envoys of God and in God's presence.

¹ **3** Does this sound like a new attempt to com- mend ourselves to you? Unlike other people, we need no letters of recommendation either to ² you or from you, ·because you are yourselves our letter, written in our hearts, that anybody can see ³ and read, ·and it is plain that you are a letter from Christ, drawn up by us, and written not with ink but with the Spirit of the living God, not on stone tablets but on the tablets of your living hearts.

⁴ Before God, we are confident of this through ⁵ Christ: ·not that we are qualified in ourselves to claim anything as our own work: all our qualifi- ⁶ cations come from God. ·He is the one who has given us the qualifications to be the administrators of this new covenant, which is not a covenant of

written letters but of the Spirit: the written letters
⁷ bring death, but the Spirit gives life. ·Now if the
administering of death, in the written letters en-
graved on stones, was accompanied by such a
brightness that the Israelites could not bear looking at the face of Moses, though it was a bright-
⁸ ness that faded, ·then how much greater will be
the brightness that surrounds the administering of
⁹ the Spirit! ·For if there was any splendor in administering condemnation, there must be very
much greater splendor in administering justifica-
¹⁰ tion. ·In fact, compared with this greater splendor, the thing that used to have such splendor
¹¹ now seems to have none; ·and if what was so temporary had any splendor, there must be much
more in what is going to last for ever.

¹²   Having this hope, we can be quite confident;
¹³ not like Moses, who put a veil over his face so
that the Israelites would not notice the ending of
¹⁴ what had to fade. ·And anyway, their minds had
been dulled; indeed, to this very day, that same
veil is still there when the old covenant is being
read, a veil never lifted, since Christ alone can
¹⁵ remove it. ·Yes, even today, whenever Moses is
¹⁶ read, the veil is over their minds. ·It will not be
¹⁷ removed until they turn to the Lord. ·Now this
Lord is the Spirit, and where the Spirit of the
¹⁸ Lord is, there is freedom. ·And we, with our unveiled faces reflecting like mirrors the brightness
of the Lord, all grow brighter and brighter as we
are turned into the image that we reflect; this is
the work of the Lord who is Spirit.

⌖

While accounting for the change in his travel plans,
Paul had responded to accusations that he was proud,
boastful and too intent on commending himself before
others (1:12,14). Since the quality of his apostolic

ministry had been attacked, he now embarks on a
major effort to describe and clarify that ministry
(2:12 – 7:16). The entire discussion is situated within
a continuing account of his travels (2:12–13, 7:5–16).
In 1:12 – 2:11, Paul had reaffirmed his plans to go to
Corinth; in 2:12 – 7:16, he indicates how, contrary to
those plans, he went to Macedonia and remained there.
Both passages emphasize how Paul's plans and their
revisions were determined by events in Corinth. The
Corinthian church is ever at the center of Paul's attention.

From Ephesus in Asia, Paul had gone to proclaim
the gospel in Troas. However, Titus' delayed return
and the long silence in Paul's communication with
Corinth moved him to abandon a successful and unhin-
dered mission in that port city and to proceed to Macedonia (2:12–13). After these introductory observations, Paul sets aside his immediate concerns in
Macedonia and embarks on a long development concerning the meaning of his ministry in general
(2:12 – 7:4). His initial observations focus on his mission in the context of a new covenant (2:14 – 3:18).

Paul and his co-workers are partners in God's tri-
umph. God reveals himself through their work, a work
which is done in Christ and which is consequently
Christ's prayerful offering to God. Comparable to in-
cense, this offering, that is Paul's work in Christ, is an
act of worship. For those who are being saved, that
offering leads to life; for those who are not being
saved, it leads to death. Of himself, Paul is not qualified for such a work, but at least he has not betrayed
his mission as God's envoy (2:14–17).

In Paul's understanding, those being saved (2:15)
are those who had been justified in baptism, whose life
was fulfilling their baptismal commitment and who

were on the way to resurrection. Those not being saved (2:15) were not living in a manner consonant with the promise of their baptism. They had accepted to die with Christ on behalf of others, but they failed to follow through on this commitment (see 1 Co 10:1–13; Rm 5:1–11, 6:2–5).

Sensitive to accusations that he was boastful (1:12,14), Paul's statement concerning his exalted mission (2:14–17) leads him to recall this accusation and forcefully to dismiss it. Paul has no need to commend himself to the Corinthians. The present letter is not a letter of self-recommendation. In fact, Paul needs no letters of recommendation whatsoever. The Corinthians themselves are his letter, a living letter which Paul had written in their hearts with the Spirit of the living God (3:1–3).

The Pauline word, which had been received and interiorized by the community, is thus manifest in the lives of all. Such a word is contrasted with a word of mere ink, as might be written in a letter, and with words inscribed on tablets of stone (3:1–3). Paul's message evokes Jr 31:31–34 and Ezk 11:19, 36:26. The former had promised a new covenant whose law would be inscribed upon the hearts of its participants. The latter had announced the divine gift of a new spirit.

The reference to Jeremiah and Ezekiel prepares the addressees for Paul's subsequent development on the nature of his ministry. Paul and his co-workers are administrators or ministers of a new covenant, a covenant of the life-giving Spirit, unlike the old covenant which brought death. It is for this that they had been qualified by God (3:4–6; see 2:16). The extraordinary quality of that ministry stands out in its full clarity when we recognize the brilliance of the Mosaic covenant. In light of the new covenant, which is eternal, the old covenant, splendid but temporary, pales and fades into nothing. What is true of these covenants also applies to their respective ministries (3:7–11).

The unit concludes with a development on 3:7b, where Paul had recalled that the Israelites had been unable to gaze upon the brilliance of Moses' features as he descended from God's presence. He now points out that Moses had veiled his face precisely so that the Israelites would not be able to observe the fading of that brilliance (3:12–13; see 3:7b). So veiled, the old covenant remains inscrutable unless Christ removes that veil, and this takes place when someone turns to the Lord, who is the Spirit of freedom from death (3:12–17).

Unlike Moses, the ministers of the new covenant are unveiled. As they increasingly reflect the brilliance of the Lord, they are progressively transformed into the image they reflect. This transformation is effected by the Lord who is the Spirit (3:18).

STUDY QUESTIONS: How are the Corinthians involved in Paul's theology of the word? What is the relationship between the two covenants? How do their ministers differ?

2 Corinthians 4:1–18
TREASURE IN A FRAGILE VESSEL

1 Since we have by an act of mercy been entrusted with this work of administration, there
2 is no weakening on our part. ·On the contrary, we will have none of the reticence of those who are ashamed, no deceitfulness or watering down the word of God; but the way we commend ourselves to every human being with a conscience is
3 by stating the truth openly in the sight of God. ·If our gospel does not penetrate the veil, then the veil is on those who are not on the way to salva-
4 tion; ·the unbelievers whose minds the god of this world has blinded, to stop them seeing the light shed by the Good News of the glory of Christ,
5 who is the image of God. ·For it is not ourselves that we are preaching, but Christ Jesus as the Lord, and ourselves as your servants for Jesus'
6 sake. ·It is the same God that said, "Let there be light shining out of darkness," who has shone in our minds to radiate the light of the knowledge of God's glory, the glory on the face of Christ.
7 We are only the earthenware jars that hold this treasure, to make it clear that such an overwhelm-
8 ing power comes from God and not from us. ·We are in difficulties on all sides, but never cornered; we see no answer to our problems, but never de-
9 spair; ·we have been persecuted, but never de-
10 serted; knocked down, but never killed; ·always, wherever we may be, we carry with us in our body the death of Jesus, so that the life of Jesus, too,
11 may always be seen in our body. ·Indeed, while we are still alive, we are consigned to our death every day, for the sake of Jesus, so that in our mortal flesh the life of Jesus, too, may be openly

¹² shown. ·So death is at work in us, but life in you.
¹³   But as we have the same spirit of faith that is
mentioned in scripture—I believed, and therefore
I spoke—we too believe and therefore we too
¹⁴ speak, ·knowing that he who raised the Lord
Jesus to life will raise us with Jesus in our turn,
¹⁵ and put us by his side and you with us. ·You see,
all this is for your benefit, so that the more grace
is multiplied among people, the more thanksgiving there will be, to the glory of God.
¹⁶   That is why there is no weakening on our part,
and instead, though this outer man of ours may
be falling into decay, the inner man is renewed
¹⁷ day by day. ·Yes, the troubles which are soon
over, though they weigh little, train us for the carrying of a weight of eternal glory which is out of
¹⁸ all proportion to them. ·And so we have no eyes
for things that are visible, but only for things that
are invisible; for visible things last only for a
time, and the invisible things are eternal.

✠

After presenting his work as a ministry of the new
covenant (2:12–3:18), entrusted to him by divine
mercy (4:1a), Paul boldly affirms that there has been
no weakening on his part, nor for that matter on the
part of Timothy (4:1b). By this he means that, unlike
some others, he has always stated the truth openly before God (4:2). If at times it appears to be otherwise,
this is not because he himself has veiled the glorious
image of God in Christ. Rather the veil is on those who
are not on the way to salvation (4:3–4; see 3:7–18).
The truth or Gospel which Paul preaches (4:2) is not
Paul's own person but Christ the Lord. Paul and his
co-workers are only servants of Jesus through whom
God reveals the glory of Christ (4:5–6). In a sense

then, Paul does preach himself, but purely as the visible expression or "sacrament" of Christ's glory.

Paul's very fragility as a living sign of Christ testifies to the divine source of his power (4:7). In 4:8–12, Paul presents the obvious indications of the fragility of the earthen vessel that he is. All his difficulties, problems and persecutions, however, are actually signs of Christ's death and new life. Like Jesus, Paul does not weaken (4:1,7), and that is why the signs of death in him lead to life for those he serves (4:12).

Paul's faith is that the sufferings he now experiences will lead to life for others and for himself, as indeed they had done in the case of Jesus (4:13–15). Ultimately that is why he does not weaken (4:16a, 4:1,7). Outwardly, he may suffer decay, but inwardly he is progressively renewed (4:16b). Accordingly his gaze is fixed on the invisible realities, which are eternal, and not on outward appearances, which are temporal (4:17–18). Paul is thus a "sacrament" of Christ's commitment and death, and so he intends to remain. His reflections on his own ministry should enable the Corinthians to understand their own sufferings, and his example should inspire them not to weaken.

STUDY QUESTIONS: In what sense can Paul be considered the object of his preaching? How does Paul interpret his weakness and fragility from a theological point of view?

2 Corinthians 5:1–10
OUR TRUE HOME

1 5 For we know that when the tent that we live
in on earth is folded up, there is a house built
by God for us, an everlasting home not made by
2 human hands, in the heavens. ·In this present
state, it is true, we groan as we wait with longing
3 to put on our heavenly home over the other; ·we
should like to be found wearing clothes and not
4 without them. ·Yes, we groan and find it a burden
being still in this tent, not that we want to strip it
off, but to put the second garment over it and to
5 have what must die taken up into life. ·This is the
purpose for which God made us, and he has given
us the pledge of the Spirit.
6   We are always full of confidence, then, when
we remember that to live in the body means to
7 be exiled from the Lord, ·going as we do by faith
8 and not by sight·—we are full of confidence, I
say, and actually want to be exiled from the body
9 and make our home with the Lord. ·Whether we
are living in the body or exiled from it, we are
10 intent on pleasing him. ·For all the truth about
us will be brought out in the law court of Christ,
and each of us will get what he deserves for the
things he did in the body, good or bad.

✠

The tension between the sufferings of this life, where
all is visible and temporal, and the glorious, eternal,
but as yet invisible life toward which we tend is an essential element of the Christian mystery, which God reveals in the Church and its ministers (4:1–18). In

5:1-10, Paul pursues his reflections on this tension. In 4:1-18, however, his primary concern had been with the difficulties and the fragility of ministers entrusted with a divine mission. In 5:1-10, he focuses chiefly on the heavenly goal. In so doing, he further develops the already rich theology of resurrection outlined in 1 Corinthians 15.

The tent of our earthly dwelling will one day be replaced by a home built by God (5:1). The tent and the house or home, which evoke temporal transience and eternal permanency, are images for our historical and heavenly conditions. As symbols for life in the body of flesh and life apart from and beyond this body, they reflect the outlook of Wisdom 1-9, whose view of immortality presupposes a distinction between man's body and soul.

Paul must consequently have come into contact with currents of Alexandrian thought, where Plato's view of the relationship between body and soul had permeated the language and thought patterns of much of the populace. This view was quite different from that which spoke of resurrection. Dependent on the ancient Semitic conception of the human being, resurrection theology did not take the distinction between body and soul into consideration. Man died progressively as a whole being, and God transformed him into new life accordingly.

In keeping with the popular Platonic view, Paul now sees our present life in the body as an exile from our true home (5:6-9). While in the body, we groan under its burden and yearn for the definitive home which God makes for us and for which we were created (5:2-5).

Though Paul is open to this new view, however, he does not altogether abandon the values inherent in the notion of resurrection. Our experience and yearning is not to be freed of our earthly tent but to take it with us into new life. The two stages of human life are like garments, and our longing is actually to put on the heavenly garment over the present garment (5:2–4). Paul thus respects the continuity between our present and future life, even as he affirms the radical newness of the life which awaits us. In 1 Co 15:35–44, he had affirmed the same values with the image of the seed that is sown and the new plant which grows from it. Inherent in both statements is the demand that we be willing to let go of the limited condition of earthly life.

The Pauline position on immortality is not a mere anthropological statement such as humanistic reflection and natural philosophy might provide. Like his earlier theology of resurrection, immortality is seen in light of biblical tradition and the Christian mystery. Our permanent dwelling will be provided by God (5:1) in fulfillment of the purpose of creation and of the pledge given us in the Spirit (5:5). In our earthly tent, we walk in faith, confident that those who please the Lord will be rewarded by Christ according to their just deserts when they come to see God (5:6–10). With this understanding of retribution, Paul integrates the present passage with his earlier statements on the full unveiled vision of God (3:7–18, 4:3–6, 18).

The need to be clothed at life's fulfillment and not to be found naked (5:3) evokes the Markan narrative of the young man who abandoned the linen shroud of his baptismal commitment and ran off naked upon being seized to die and to be buried with Jesus (Mk 14:51–52).

STUDY QUESTIONS: How do the concepts of immortality and resurrection differ? How are they related? What are the elements of faith in Paul's view of immortality?

2 Corinthians 5:11 – 6:10
AMBASSADORS FOR CHRIST

¹¹ And so it is with the fear of the Lord in mind that we try to win people over. God knows us for what we really are, and I hope that in your ¹² consciences you know us too. ·This is not another attempt to commend ourselves to you: we are simply giving you reasons to be proud of us, so that you will have an answer ready for the people who can boast more about what they seem than what ¹³ they are. ·If we seemed out of our senses, it was for God; but if we are being reasonable now, it ¹⁴ is for your sake. ·And this is because the love of Christ overwhelms us when we reflect that if one man has died for all, then all men should be ¹⁵ dead; ·and the reason he died for all was so that living men should live no longer for themselves, but for him who died and was raised to life for them.

¹⁶ From now onward, therefore, we do not judge anyone by the standards of the flesh. Even if we did once know Christ in the flesh, that is not how ¹⁷ we know him now. ·And for anyone who is in Christ, there is a new creation; the old creation ¹⁸ has gone, and now the new one is here. ·It is all God's work. It was God who reconciled us to himself through Christ and gave us the work of ¹⁹ handing on this reconciliation. ·In other words, God in Christ was reconciling the world to himself, not holding men's faults against them, and he has entrusted to us the news that they are rec- ²⁰ onciled. ·So we are ambassadors for Christ; it is as though God were appealing through us, and the appeal that we make in Christ's name is: be ²¹ reconciled to God. ·For our sake God made the sinless one into sin, so that in him we might be- ¹ come the goodness of God. **6** As his fellow

workers, we beg you once again not to neglect
2 the grace of God that you have received. ·For he
says: At the favorable time, I have listened to
you; on the day of salvation I came to your help.
Well, now is the favorable time; this is the day
of salvation.
3   We do nothing that people might object to, so
as not to bring discredit on our function as God's
4 servants. ·Instead, we prove we are servants of
God by great fortitude in times of suffering: in
5 times of hardship and distress; ·when we are
flogged, or sent to prison, or mobbed; laboring,
6 sleepless, starving. ·We prove we are God's servants by our purity, knowledge, patience and
kindness; by a spirit of holiness, by a love free
7 from affectation; ·by the word of truth and by
the power of God; by being armed with the weapons of righteousness in the right hand and in the
8 left, ·prepared for honor or disgrace, for blame
or praise; taken for impostors while we are genu-
9 ine; ·obscure yet famous; said to be dying and
here are we alive; rumored to be executed before
10 we are sentenced; ·thought most miserable and
yet we are always rejoicing; taken for paupers
though we make others rich, for people having
nothing though we have everything.

✠

After presenting himself as a fragile but faithful minister of the new covenant (2:12 – 3:18) whose faith is
fixed on the eternal home which awaits him (5:1–10),
Paul goes on to describe his ministry as one of reconciliation in which he is Christ's ambassador
(5:11 – 6:10).
Once again Paul affirms the intention which moti-
vates his apostolic work, and he hopes for understanding from the Corinthians (5:11). He is not trying

to commend himself to his addressees. However, there are sound reasons why they should be proud of him. Paul is what he claims to be, unlike those who only appear such and have no genuine grounds for boasting (5:12).

As before (2:17, 4:2), Paul disassociates himself from those whose apostolic work lacks grounding in the quality of their Christian commitment. In so doing, he rejects the accusation that he had been merely trying to gain men's favor (see 1:12,14, 3:1–3). Paul's mission and all that he does and suffers are patterned on Christ who died that others might live, not for themselves, but for Christ in whom all die and live (5:13–15).

Since Christ no longer is known in the flesh but in his risen state as a new creation, the standard for judging anyone must no longer be that of the flesh (5:16–17). That standard is the very nature of God's work in and through Christ, and that work is one of reconciliation. It continues through those whom God has called to join Christ in life and mission (5:18–19). In that work, Paul does not stand independently of Christ, as though Christ had been the first of a series of reconcilers. Rather, he is Christ's ambassador in history. Paul's appeal for reconciliation is thus spoken in Christ's name (5:20–21). Writing to the Corinthians, Paul calls for fidelity to the gift of reconciliation which they already had received (6:1). Their salvation had not been definitively assured in the past. Nor is it purely a matter of the future. Now is the time for engaging in its development process (6:2).

In 6:3–10, Paul describes how in the midst of sufferings and difficulties (6:4b–5) and of false accusations, groundless blame and persecution (6:8–10), he and his fellow workers reveal themselves true and faithful

servants of God (6:3–4a,6–7). This theme of suffering
and persecution and its meaningfulness had already
been announced in the thanksgiving unit (1:3–11) and
developed as Paul gave reasons for delaying his trip to
Corinth (1:12–2:11) as well as in his reflections on
the human fragility of the minister (4:7–18). This last
unit had also been meant as a demonstration of his servanthood (4:5).

STUDY QUESTIONS: How is Paul's mission related to
that of Christ? How does the Chris-
tian work of reconciliation continue
in the world today?

11 Corinthians, we have spoken to you very frankly; our mind has been opened in front of 12 you. ·Any constraint that you feel is not on our 13 side; the constraint is in your own selves. ·I speak as if to children of mine: as a fair exchange, open your minds in the same way.

14 Do not harness yourselves in an uneven team with unbelievers. Virtue is no companion for crime. Light and darkness have nothing in com- 15 mon. ·Christ is not the ally of Beliar, nor has a believer anything to share with an unbeliever. 16 The temple of God has no common ground with idols, and that is what we are—the temple of the living God. We have God's word for it: I will make my home among them and live with them; I will be their God and they shall be my people. 17 Then come away from them and keep aloof, says the Lord. Touch nothing that is unclean, and I 18 will welcome you ·and be your father, and you shall be my sons and daughters, says the Al- mighty Lord.

1 7 With promises like these made to us, dear brothers, let us wash off all that can soil either body or spirit, to reach perfection of holiness in the fear of God.

2 Keep a place for us in your hearts. We have not injured anyone, or ruined anyone, or ex- 3 ploited anyone. ·I am not saying this to put any blame on you; as I have already told you, you are in our hearts—together we live or together we 4 die. ·I have the very greatest confidence in you, and I am so proud of you that in all our trouble

I am filled with consolation and my joy is over-
flowing.

✠

Concluding this long statement on the meaning and
purpose of his ministry and of the factors which affect
it (2:14 – 7:4), Paul reflects on all that he has just said
and draws out its implications for the Corinthians
(6:11 – 7:4). The Corinthians should receive Paul's
frank and open presentation of his work with equal
openness and fairness (6:11–13). They should thus
disassociate themselves from all who in effect are unbelievers (6:14–15), from all those who appear to be
Christians, but whose work is self-seeking and a distor-
tion of God's gospel truth (see 2:17, 4:2, 5:12).
These are the ones who have been accusing Paul and
have tried to turn the community against him. In his
defense, Paul thus means to turn the tables against
those who are not true servants by placing the accusations they had leveled against him at their own door-
step.

If the Corinthians are on the side of virtue, light and
Christ, they can have nothing to do with these men
who are unbelievers, walking in darkness and allies of
Beliar (6:14–15). Those who are the temple of the living God can have no relationship to idols, that is, to
those who usurp the place of God and Christ instead of
being their ministers, servants and ambassadors in the
reconciling ministry of the new covenant, whose apostles are not the glorious light of Christ but its reflection
(6:16a). In the Scriptures, God had promised that he
would establish his presence among his people and that
they would be his sons and daughters (6:16b–18). The

Corinthians must cleanse themselves of everything which would prevent them from arriving at the holiness and perfection which fulfills these promises (7:11).

Paul's exhortation (6:14 – 7:1) then moves into a plea for loving unity between himself and the church he had established. He had been a faithful servant (7:2). May they keep him in their hearts as they were in his, as together they live and die (7:1a,3).

At this point, Paul's response to the initial negative reaction to his letter yields to the more recent news which Titus had brought him. The unit concludes with an exuberant affirmation of pride in those who had brought him consolation and joy in the midst of the troubles he faced in Macedonia (7:4; see 1:3–7).

STUDY QUESTIONS: What does Paul mean by idols? What role do the Corinthians play in the fulfillment of God's promises?

2 Corinthians 7:5-16
RENEWED CONFIDENCE

5 Even after we had come to Macedonia, however, there was no rest for this body of ours. Far from it; we found trouble on all sides: quarrels
6 outside, misgivings inside. ·But God comforts the miserable, and he comforted us, by the arrival of
7 Titus, ·and not only by his arrival but also by the comfort which he had gained from you. He has told us all about how you want to see me, how sorry you were, and how concerned for me, and so I am happier now than I was before.
8 But to tell the truth, even if I distressed you by my letter, I do not regret it. I did regret it before, and I see that that letter did distress you, at least
9 for a time; ·but I am happy now—not because I made you suffer, but because your suffering led to your repentance. Yours has been a kind of suffering that God approves, and so you have come to
10 no kind of harm from us. ·To suffer in God's way means changing for the better and leaves no regrets, but to suffer as the world knows suffering
11 brings death. ·Just look at what suffering in God's way has brought you: what keenness, what explanations, what indignation, what alarm! Yes, and what aching to see me, what concern for me, and what justice done! In every way you have
12 shown yourselves blameless in this affair. ·So then, though I wrote the letter to you, it was not written for the sake either of the offender or of the one offended; it was to make you realize, in
13 the sight of God, your own concern for us. ·That is what we have found so encouraging.

With this encouragement, too, we had the even greater happiness of finding Titus so happy;

14 thanks to you all, he has no more worries; ·I had
rather boasted to him about you, and now I have
not been made to look foolish; in fact, our boasting to Titus has proved to be as true as anything
15 that we ever said to you. ·His own personal affection for you is all the greater when he remembers
how willing you have all been, and with what deep
16 respect you welcomed him. ·I am very happy
knowing that I can rely on you so completely.

⊞

In this last section (7:5–16) of the first part
(1:12 – 7:16) of his letter, Paul returns to some of the
concerns developed in 1:12 – 2:11 and 2:12–13. Once
again, he takes up the matter of the letter which had
distressed the Corinthians (7:8–12; see 2:3–4), his
present situation in Macedonia (7:5; see 1:16,
2:12–13) and the mission of Titus (7:6–7,13b–16; see
2:13).

Literarily, 2 Co 7:5 takes up the account of the
journey to Troas and from Troas to Macedonia which
Paul had introduced in 2:12–13. With regard to this
continuous narrative, the section on Paul's apostolic
ministry (2:14 – 7:4) stands as a long but extremely
important digression. We may safely assume that
2:14 – 7:4 was based on Paul's previous reflection on
his ministry and that he had now developed and applied that reflection to the actual conditions at Corinth
and to his relationship to that church. We can thus understand how much of what is said does not reflect the
good news brought by Titus just prior to Paul's writing
of 2 Corinthians. In spite of the recently ameliorated
situation, Paul found it necessary to respond to the
negative reaction which first greeted his previous letter.

With Titus' arrival, Paul finds himself comforted in

the midst of the troubles which afflicted him in Macedonia (7:5–6). Part of his comfort stems from the way the Corinthians have comforted Titus himself, but its main source is Titus' news of the Corinthians' desire for reconciliation with Paul. Sorry for the pain they had caused him and genuinely concerned, they now want to see him again (7:7).

Reflecting on this earlier letter, Paul then states that he had been sorry concerning the distress it had caused, but no longer. Suffering which leads to repentance is no cause for regret. Such suffering is divinely approved and productive of good. It must be distinguished from the empty suffering of this world which is meaningless and brings death (7:8–11). The letter has benefited the whole community. It had been meant for the offended as well as for the offender (7:12–13).

Paul is especially happy over Titus' new relationship to the community. Paul had boasted to him about the Corinthians and his boasting had not been empty (7:13b–16). This concluding reference to boasting on behalf of others reflects Paul's confidence that all accusations leveled against him as a boaster are now safely laid to rest (1:12,14, 3:1–3, 5:12). May Paul be their boast (1:14) as they were his (7:14).

STUDY QUESTIONS: Is all suffering meaningful? Why does Paul mention that he had boasted concerning the Corinthians?

2 Corinthians 8:1–15
THE COLLECTION FOR THE SAINTS

¹ 8 Now here, brothers, is the news of the grace of God which was given in the churches in
² Macedonia; ·and of how, throughout great trials by suffering, their constant cheerfulness and their intense poverty have overflowed in a wealth of
³ generosity. ·I can swear that they gave not only as much as they could afford, but far more, and
⁴ quite spontaneously, ·begging and begging us for the favor of sharing in this service to the saints
⁵ and, what was quite unexpected, they offered their own selves first to God and, under God, to us.
⁶ Because of this, we have asked Titus, since he has already made a beginning, to bring this work of mercy to the same point of success among you.
⁷ You always have the most of everything—of faith, of eloquence, of understanding, of keenness for any cause, and the biggest share of our affection— so we expect you to put the most into this work of
⁸ mercy too. ·It is not an order that I am giving you; I am just testing the genuineness of your love
⁹ against the keenness of others. ·Remember how generous the Lord Jesus was: he was rich, but he became poor for your sake, to make you rich
¹⁰ out of his poverty. ·As I say, I am only making a suggestion; it is only fair to you, since you were the first, a year ago, not only in taking action but
¹¹ even in deciding to. ·So now finish the work and let the results be worthy, as far as you can afford
¹² it, of the decision you made so promptly. ·As long as the readiness is there, a man is acceptable with whatever he can afford; never mind what is be-
¹³ yond his means. ·This does not mean that to give

relief to others you ought to make things difficult
14 for yourselves: it is a question of balancing ·what
happens to be your surplus now against their present need, and one day they may have something
to spare that will supply your own need. That is
15 how we strike a balance: ·as scripture says: The
man who gathered much had none too much, the
man who gathered little did not go short.

✠

The second part of the letter (8:1 – 9:15) concerns
the collection which Paul has been organizing in the
Aegean provinces and in Galatia (1 Co 16:1) for the
poor of Jerusalem and Judaea (1:17). In 1 Corinthians 16, this collection was clearly associated with
Paul's travel plans (1 Co 16:1–4,5–9). The same is
true of the present long development, which immediately follows 1:12 – 7:16. Since Paul cannot go to
Corinth at the present time, Titus and others will precede him (8:6) and prepare his visit (9:4–5).

Throughout the second part of the letter, Paul reveals his ongoing concern for the church in Macedonia
(8:1–5, 9:1–5), from which he is writing. His work
and the situation in Macedonia had also framed Paul's
long statement (2:12 – 7:16) on his apostolic ministry
(2:12–13, 7:5). Through Paul's word and work,
the Macedonian and Achaian communities gradually
learned to see themselves as members of the larger
Christian movement. The collection itself provided a
concrete means of expressing their relationship to the
emerging universal Church.

Paul begins by imparting news concerning the Gospel at work in Macedonia and the success of the collection in that province (8:1–5). He is extremely proud

of these Macedonian churches for whom suffering and
poverty have been no hindrance. While boasting to the
Achaian churches concerning the Macedonians
(8:1–5), he also boasts to the latter concerning the
Christians of Corinth and Achaia (9:2).

Titus, who already had made one successful trip to
Corinth (7:5–16) is commissioned to oversee the collection in that city (8:6). By God's mercy, the
Corinthians have been blessed with an abundance of
gifts; may they show like mercy to those who are in
need (8:7–8). In this they have the example of Christ,
who was rich but who became poor that through his
poverty we might become rich (8:9). Christ's relin-
quishing of divine richness to become humanly poor is
the theme of the hymn which Paul cites in Ph 2:6–11.
This hymn, which articulates the paradox of suffering
and the Cross, seems to have influenced Paul's basic
thinking and is frequently reflected in the theology of
his letters.

Since the original initiative to launch the collection
had come from the Corinthians themselves, Paul has
no need to convince them in the matter but only to sug-
gest a generous follow-through (8:8,10–11). In doing
so, he provides important normative guidelines for
charitable giving. The Christians are not asked to give
beyond what they can afford but only what corresponds to their means. Little would be gained if they
were to impoverish themselves (8:11–13). In such
matters, they must strike a balance. Some day the same
would work in their favor (8:13–15).

STUDY QUESTIONS: What is the rhetorical effect of
Paul's boasting concerning the gen-
erosity of the poor churches of
Macedonia? How does Christ pro-

vide a model for those who are asked to give to the collection? Can Paul's guidelines for charitable giving be misapplied? How does the totality of Paul's statement in 8:1–15 obviate any misinterpretation or twisting of his norms?

2 Corinthians 8:16 – 9:5
TITUS AND HIS COMPANIONS

16 I thank God for putting into Titus' heart the
17 same concern for you that I have myself. ·He did
what we asked him; indeed he is more concerned
than ever, and is visiting you on his own initiative.
18 As his companion we are sending the brother
who is famous in all the churches for spreading
19 the gospel. ·More than that, he happens to be
the same brother who has been elected by the
churches to be our companion on this errand of
mercy that, for the glory of God, we have under-
20 taken to satisfy our impatience to help. ·We hope
that in this way there will be no accusations made
21 about our administering such a large fund; ·for
we are trying to do right not only in the sight
22 of God but also in the sight of men. ·To accompany these, we are sending a third brother, of
whose keenness we have often had proof in many
different ways, and who is particularly keen about
23 this, because he has great confidence in you. ·Ti-
tus, perhaps I should add, is my own colleague
and fellow worker in your interests; the other two
brothers, who are delegates of the churches, are
24 a real glory to Christ. ·So then, in front of all the
churches, give them a proof of your love, and
prove to them that we are right to be proud of
you.

9 1 There is really no need for me to write to you
on the subject of offering your services to
2 the saints, ·since I know how anxious you are to
help; in fact, I boast about you to the Macedonians, telling them, "Achaia has been ready
since last year." So your zeal has been a spur to
3 many more. ·I am sending the brothers all the

same, to make sure that our boasting about you
does not prove to have been empty this time, and
that you really are ready as I said you would be.
⁴ If some of the Macedonians who are coming with
me found you unprepared, we should be humiliated—to say nothing of yourselves—after being
⁵ so confident. •That is why I have thought it necessary to ask these brothers to go on to you ahead
of us, and make sure in advance that the gift you
promised is all ready, and that it all comes as a
gift out of your generosity and not by being ex-
torted from you.

✠

Since Titus shares Paul's love for the Corinthians, he
is a good choice to undertake this mission. Actually,
the initiative to go came from Titus himself (8:16–17).
To accompany Titus, who was Paul's personal envoy
(8:23a), the churches had delegated two other
men whose Christian credentials were impeccable
(8:18–19,22,23b). The generosity of the Corinthians
would thus be a response not to Paul alone but to the
other churches (8:24). For his part, Paul was well
protected against any accusations of impropriety or
mismanagement (8:20). Even the appearance of evil
would thus be obviated (8:21).

The above program for managing a major Christian
collection and handling its funds seems eminently wise
and provides a model for similar collections in our day.
The reasons for launching it and the motivation of
those who engaged in it are no less exemplary.

Although Paul finds it unnecessary to elaborate on
the need to contribute to the collection, he does mar-
shal all the elements of an impressive exhortation.
Even his mention that he has no need to write is horta-

tory. Besides, however, he reminds them of how he had boasted concerning them to the Macedonians. Would not Paul and they themselves be humiliated when Paul and some Macedonian brothers arrived in Corinth, should nothing have been prepared beforehand? That is the reason some have been sent in advance of Paul's visit. The section ends with a subtle reference to the Corinthians' promise and generosity. Paul leaves nothing to chance. He does indeed love the Corinthians, but he has also had some bitter and disappointing experiences with them.

STUDY QUESTIONS: How does Paul use human wisdom and ingenuity to assure a successful collection? How does the composition of the Macedonian delegation contribute to the development of a universal Christianity which transcends the life and work of Paul?

2 Corinthians 9:6–15
GIVING AND RECEIVING

⁶ Do not forget: thin sowing means thin reap- ⁷ ing; the more you sow, the more you reap. ·Each one should give what he has decided in his own mind, not grudgingly or because he is made to, ⁸ for God loves a cheerful giver. ·And there is no limit to the blessings which God can send you—he will make sure that you will always have all you need for yourselves in every possible circum- stance, and still have something to spare for all ⁹ sorts of good works. ·As scripture says: He was free in almsgiving, and gave to the poor: his good deeds will never be forgotten.

¹⁰ "The one who provides seed for the sower and bread for food will provide you with all the seed you want and make the harvest of your good ¹¹ deeds a larger one, ·and, made richer in every way, you will be able to do all the generous things which, through us, are the cause of thanksgiving ¹² to God. ·For doing this holy service is not only supplying all the needs of the saints, but it is also increasing the amount of thanksgiving that God ¹³ receives. ·By offering this service, you show them what you are, and that makes them give glory to God for the way you accept and profess the gospel of Christ, and for your sympathetic generosity ¹⁴ to them and to all. ·And their prayers for you, too, show how they are drawn to you on account of ¹⁵ all the grace that God has given you. ·Thanks be to God for his inexpressible gift!

✠

In 9:6–15, Paul returns to the themes of wealth and poverty and of giving and receiving which formed the

basis of 8:1–15. As he noted in 8:14–15, giving leads
to receiving. The image of sowing and reaping, which
Paul used to describe the resurrection (1 Co
15:36–38) and his own work at Corinth (1 Co 3:6–9)
is now applied to charitable giving in the present and to
the bountiful help and blessings which will come from
it. Those who plant generously will harvest abundantly.
While Paul appears to be describing a situation of fact,
his intention throughout the unit is definitely hortatory.

As the second part of the letter comes to its
confident and grateful conclusion (9:15), Paul situates
the collection in theological perspective (9:10–15).
God is at the origins, development and conclusion of
the whole enterprise. He it is who provides both the
seed which is planted and the bread which comes from
the harvest (9:10). Images aside, the abundance which
the Corinthians have received and their act of sharing
(the seed) is God's gift. So is the generous response
(the harvest) which the Corinthians will receive when
they too are in need. As the instruments of God's
munificence, they also contribute to the thanksgiving
which God will receive. The greater their gift to others,
the greater will be the thanksgiving (9:11–12). Not
only that, but their generosity manifests the Christian
Gospel, and all who see it are led to give glory to God
(9:13). These same people will surely pray for the
Corinthians (9:14).

The collection is thus a source of thanksgiving, ado-
ration and prayer, all three of which demonstrate God's
gift and call for gratitude (9:15).

STUDY QUESTIONS: How does Paul use the image of
sowing and reaping? How is the
collection related to the dynamics
of worship?

2 Corinthians 10:1–11
PLANS TO VISIT CORINTH

1 **10** This is a personal matter; this is Paul himself appealing to you by the gentleness and patience of Christ—I, the man who is so humble when he is facing you, but bullies you when he is
2 at a distance. ·I only ask that I do not have to bully you when I come, with all the confident assurance I mean to show when I come face to face with people I could name who think we go by
3 ordinary human motives. ·We live in the flesh, of course, but the muscles that we fight with are
4 not flesh. ·Our war is not fought with weapons of flesh, yet they are strong enough, in God's cause, to demolish fortresses. We demolish soph-
5 istries, ·and the arrogance that tries to resist the knowledge of God; every thought is our prisoner, captured to be brought into obedience to Christ.
6 Once you have given your complete obedience, we are prepared to punish any disobedience.

7 Face plain facts. Anybody who is convinced that he belongs to Christ must go on to reflect that we all belong to Christ no less than he does.
8 Maybe I do boast rather too much about our authority, but the Lord gave it to me for building you up and not for pulling you down, and I shall
9 not be ashamed of it. ·I do not want you to think of me as someone who only frightens you by
10 letter. ·Someone said, "He writes powerful and strongly worded letters but when he is with you you see only half a man and no preacher at all."
11 The man who said that can remember this: whatever we are like in the words of our letters when we are absent, that is what we shall be like in our actions when we are present.

✠

In the third and final part of the letter
(10:1 – 13:13), Paul returns to the major theme already developed in the first part (1:12 – 7:6), that is
the defense of his apostleship. In this section, however,
he is more concerned with comparisons that have been
made between himself and others, whom he satirically
categorizes as archapostles, and with disassociating
himself from such people. Part one had also been more
theological than this third part, which includes elements for a theology of ministry but which is far more
in the form of a personal defense or apologia.

Leaving the final greeting and blessing aside
(13:11–13), the section is beautifully structured.
Seven units can be discerned in which the first, second
and third correspond to the seventh, sixth and fifth, in
that order. At the heart of this development, which sets
out Paul's plans to visit Corinth (10:1–11,
12:19 – 13:10; see 1:12 – 2:11 and 7:5–16), com-
pares Paul to the so-called archapostles (10:12 – 11:6,
12:11–18) and recalls Paul's history at Corinth and
earlier (11:7–15, 12:1–10), Paul presents his view of
Christian boasting in the Lord (11:16–33). This structure, which is known as a chiasm, provides the entire
section with a strong sense of order and movement in
which communication with the Corinthians is never
displaced by the subject being treated.

Paul's attitude in this section is far more severe than
that which was noted in chapters 8 and 9. This seeming
contradiction in Paul's attitude can be explained by his
rhetorical mode of writing, in which the reaction of his
readers is a more basic consideration than the material

objectivity of his statements and his attitudinal consistency. Paul is not only expressing himself. He means to evoke and shape an attitude in his readers. Accordingly, with regard to the collection, he was gently hortatory; with regard to his apostleship, he is determined, uncompromising and at times satirical.

The present passage (10:1–11) begins and ends with an appeal couched in a satirical reference to statements made concerning him as unable to face the Corinthians with the same strength which he demonstrated while away from them (10:1,9–11). Paul warns his readers that when he does come they will witness the strength and assurance which they recognized in his letters (10:2,11).

Between these opening and closing statements (10:1–2 and 9–11), Paul affirms that his strength in fighting sophistries and arrogance is not from the flesh but from Christ (10:3–8). Having given his total obedience to Christ, he is ready to confront any disobedience (10:6) in those who deny his Christian allegiance (10:7).

STUDY QUESTIONS: What is the structure of 10:1–13:10? How can we account for the difference in Paul's attitude between 8:1–9:15 and 10:1–13:10? What is the nature of the accusation which some have leveled against Paul?

2 Corinthians 10:12 – 11:6
PAUL AND THE ARCHAPOSTLES

¹² We are not being so bold as to rank ourselves, or invite comparison, with certain people who write their own references. Measuring themselves against themselves, and comparing them- ¹³ selves to themselves, they are simply foolish. ·We, on the other hand, are not going to boast without a standard to measure against: taking for our measure the yardstick which God gave us to measure with, which is long enough to reach to ¹⁴ you. ·We are not stretching further than we ought; otherwise we should not have reached you, as we did come all the way to you with the ¹⁵ gospel of Christ. ·So we are not boasting without any measure, about work that was done by other people; in fact, we trust that, as your faith grows, we shall get taller and taller, when judged by our ¹⁶ own standard. ·I mean, we shall be carrying the gospel to places far beyond you, without en- croaching on anyone else's field, not boasting of ¹⁷ the work already done. ·If anyone wants to boast, ¹⁸ let him boast of the Lord. ·It is not the man who commends himself that can be accepted, but the man who is commended by the Lord.

¹ 11 I only wish you were able to tolerate a little foolishness from me. But of course: you ² are tolerant toward me. ·You see, the jealousy that I feel for you is God's own jealousy: I ar- ranged for you to marry Christ so that I might give you away as a chaste virgin to this one hus- ³ band. ·But the serpent, with his cunning, seduced Eve, and I am afraid that in the same way your ideas may get corrupted and turned away from ⁴ simple devotion to Christ. ·Because any new-

comer has only to proclaim a new Jesus, different
from the one that we preached, or you have only
to receive a new spirit, different from the one
you have already received, or a new gospel, different from the one you have already accepted—and
5 you welcome it with open arms. ·As far as I can
tell, these archapostles have nothing more than I
6 have. ·I may not be a polished speechmaker, but
as for knowledge, that is a different matter; surely
we have made this plain, speaking on every subject in front of all of you.

✠

Paul now attacks the way he has been compared to
other apostles, which he sarcastically refers to as archapostles (11:5). These men have no standard or
measure outside of themselves which would allow for a
genuine appraisal of their worth (10:12). For Paul,
the ultimate criterion is the Gospel of Christ, which led
him to reach across the miles all the way to Corinth.
Concretely, that standard is now the very life of the
Corinthians in whom the Gospel has been inscribed
(10:13–15). We thus have a fresh statement of the
theology of the Gospel word which had been presented
in 3:1–3.

Paul would travel far beyond Corinth in the service
of the Gospel. The broadening scope of his work
would reveal his true stature, which looms far higher
than that of those whose Gospel vision is more limited
(10:16–18).

In this development, Paul includes one of the basic
principles of his mission, which is to preach in areas
where the Gospel has not yet been heard. In this way,
he does not encroach on anyone else's work. This
statement must be read as a subtle accusation directed

at those who consider themselves superior to Paul in
the ongoing Corinthian mission (10:16–18).

In 11:1–2, Paul asks for tolerance and defends his
apostolic jealousy. He has not acquired the Corinthian
community for himself but for Christ, and he has presented it to Christ. The cunning, seductive serpent,
however, is now threatening the community's very relationship to Christ (11:3). That serpent is working
through those who are preaching a new Gospel and
giving a new spirit, different from those which came
through Paul (11:4). These archapostles may be superior to Paul in oral delivery, but in knowledge they
clearly have nothing more than he has (11:5–6).

STUDY QUESTIONS: What criterion does Paul use to
evaluate his apostolic work? What
does he mean by jealousy? How is
his jealousy justified?

2 Corinthians 11:7–15
PAUL AT CORINTH

7 Or was I wrong, lowering myself so as to lift you high, by preaching the gospel of God to you 8 and taking no fee for it? ·I was robbing other churches, living on them so that I could serve 9 you. ·When I was with you and ran out of money, I was no burden to anyone; the brothers who came from Macedonia provided me with everything I wanted. I was very careful, and I always shall be, not to be a burden to you in 10 any way, ·and by Christ's truth in me, this cause of boasting will never be taken from me in the 11 regions of Achaia. ·Would I do that if I did not 12 love you? God knows I do. ·I intend to go on doing what I am doing now—leaving no opportunity for those people who are looking for an opportunity to claim equality with us in what they 13 boast of. ·These people are counterfeit apostles, they are dishonest workmen disguised as apostles 14 of Christ. ·There is nothing unexpected about that; if Satan himself goes disguised as an angel 15 of light, ·there is no need to be surprised when his servants, too, disguise themselves as the servants of righteousness. They will come to the end that they deserve.

✠

Paul now turns to his personal history at Corinth and the concrete way he had gone about preaching the Gospel. The public demeanor and way of life of the archapostles (11:5) is obviously quite different from that of Paul. Was Paul's simple and humble way, in which he saw to his own livelihood and refrained from imposing on the Corinthians, a mistake? It certainly was being construed to his detriment (11:7-10). The passage evokes his response to those who had come to him from Chloe in 1 Co 1:10 – 4:21 and in particular his application of the Gospel of the Cross to the weak and non-influential condition of the Corinthians (1:26-31) and to his own life as a missionary (2:1-5).

Responding to what appear to be the expectations of the Corinthians, Paul then affirms his intention to continue to act as before. He had acted out of love for them, and he would continue to do so. Were these not grounds for boasting (11:11-12)? Those who take a fee for their Gospel service, on the other hand, are counterfeit apostles (11:7,13). They are servants of Satan, whose disguise is no less clever than that of their master (11:14-15a).

As servants of Satan, they will receive the reward which corresponds to their service (11:15b)!

STUDY QUESTIONS: What seems to be the main difference between Paul's Gospel service and that of the counterfeit apostles? What grounds does Paul provide for boasting about his mission?

¹⁶ As I said before, let no one take me for a fool; but if you must, then treat me as a fool and ¹⁷ let me do a little boasting of my own. ·What I am going to say now is not prompted by the Lord, but said as if in a fit of folly, in the cer- ¹⁸ tainty that I have something to boast about. ·So many others have been boasting of their worldly ¹⁹ achievements, that I will boast myself. ·You are all wise men and can cheerfully tolerate fools, ²⁰ yes, even to tolerating somebody who makes slaves of you, makes you feed him, imposes on you, orders you about and slaps you in the face. ²¹ I hope you are ashamed of us for being weak with you instead!

But if anyone wants some brazen speaking—I am still talking as a fool—then I can be as brazen ²² as any of them, and about the same things. ·He- brews, are they? So am I. Israelites? So am I. ²³ Descendants of Abraham? So am I. ·The ser- vants of Christ? I must be mad to say this, but so am I, and more than they: more, because I have worked harder, I have been sent to prison more often, and whipped so many times more, ²⁴ often almost to death. ·Five times I had the ²⁵ thirty-nine lashes from the Jews; ·three times I have been beaten with sticks; once I was stoned; three times I have been shipwrecked and once adrift in the open sea for a night and a day. ²⁶ Constantly traveling, I have been in danger from rivers and in danger from brigands, in danger from my own people and in danger from pagans; in danger in the towns, in danger in the open country, danger at sea and danger from so-called

²⁷ brothers. ·I have worked and labored, often
without sleep; I have been hungry and thirsty
and often starving; I have been in the cold with-
²⁸ out clothes. ·And, to leave out much more, there
is my daily preoccupation: my anxiety for all
²⁹ the churches. ·When any man has had scruples,
I have had scruples with him; when any man is
made to fall, I am tortured.

³⁰   If I am to boast, then let me boast of my own
³¹ feebleness. ·The God and Father of the Lord
Jesus—bless him for ever—knows that I am not
³² lying. ·When I was in Damascus, the ethnarch of
King Aretas put guards around the city to catch
³³ me, ·and I had to be let down over the wall in a
hamper, through a window, in order to escape.

✠

Since Paul is taken for a fool, he will speak like a
fool, and he expects his boasting to be received accordingly. After all, the Corinthians are wise men. They
should be able to recognize foolish talk and accept it as
such. Had they not tolerated the fools who enslaved
them and depended on them for their sustenance?
Surely they have a right to be ashamed of the weakness
which Paul had demonstrated with them (11:16–21a).
Rarely is Paul so bitingly satirical or rhetorically effective. Were his word not spoken out of love and with a
view to shocking the Corinthians into recognizing how
foolish they are in their wisdom, the passage would
leave us feeling uneasy. Like 11:7, the unit continues
to evoke Paul's earlier statement in 1 Co 1:26–2:5.

In his boasting, Paul begins by comparing his origins
and mission as an Israelite, a descendant of Abraham
and a servant of Christ to those of the counterfeit or
superapostles (11:21b–23a). As a servant of Christ,

he surpasses all the others because he has suffered
more and worked harder (11:23b–29). His boast thus
moves from the glory of his origins as a Jew and his
mission as a Christian to the suffering and weakness
which have characterized his work. In so doing, he
demonstrates the true basis for Christian boasting.
Once again we see how human weakness reveals the
strength of God. God's wisdom shines through human
folly when it is allied with the folly of the Cross.

Placing aside all foolish talk, Paul then articulates
what he has just demonstrated. His only true boast is
his feebleness (11:30). In conclusion, Paul supports
this statement by recalling the incident in Damascus
when he had to be lowered over the wall in a basket to
escape the local representative of King Aretas. Aretas
was ruler of the Nabataean kingdom, whose capital
was at Petra in the region known as Arabia. During
this period, Damascus fell within the sway of Nabataean power.

STUDY QUESTIONS: What did Paul mean to achieve by
his use of language in 11:16–21a?
What is the content of Paul's boasting, and what was its purpose?

2 Corinthians 12:1–10
VISION, REVELATION AND CONVERSION

1 **12** Must I go on boasting, though there is nothing to be gained by it? But I will move on to the visions and revelations I have 2 had from the Lord. ·I know a man in Christ who, fourteen years ago, was caught up—whether still in the body or out of the body, I do not know; God knows—right into the third heaven. 3 I do know, however, that this same person—whether in the body or out of the body, I do not 4 know; God knows—·was caught up into paradise and heard things which must not and cannot 5 be put into human language. ·I will boast about a man like that, but not about anything of my 6 own except my weaknesses. ·If I should decide to boast, I should not be made to look foolish, because I should only be speaking the truth; but I am not going to, in case anyone should begin to think I am better than he can actually see and hear me to be.

7 In view of the extraordinary nature of these revelations, to stop me from geting too proud I was given a thorn in the flesh, an angel of Satan to beat me and stop me from getting too proud! 8 About this thing, I have pleaded with the Lord 9 three times for it to leave me, ·but he has said, "My grace is enough for you: my power is at its best in weakness." So I shall be very happy to make my weaknesses my special boast so that 10 the power of Christ may stay over me, ·and that is why I am quite content with my weaknesses, and with insults, hardships, persecutions, and the agonies I go through for Christ's sake. For it is when I am weak that I am strong.

✠

Paul now continues with the personal history which he had begun in 11:7–15. In the previous unit, he had focused on his envagelization of Corinth. In 12:1–10, he leaps beyond that mission and discusses the visions and revelations which accompanied his conversion to Christ and the Christian mission. Visions and revelations must be viewed as two distinct designations for the same experiential event. In 1 Co 15:8, Paul had described this event as an appearance of Christ; in Ga 1:12 and 16, he had presented it as God's revelation of Jesus Christ to him. For Paul, auditory and visual terms are thus used to point to a reality which transcends them both.

In the unit's first section (12:1–6), he refers to himself in the third person, as though he were describing someone else's experience, as well as in the first person (12:2–5a,5b–6). Far more than a literary artifice, this device has profound theological significance. In his conversion, Paul, the man he knows of fourteen years ago, was graced by God in an altogether extraordinary and gratuitous manner, for which he can claim no responsibility but for which he has every reason to boast in the Lord. The experience actually defies description and limited human language (12:2–5a). With regard to his subsequent life, however, and his correspondence to the grace which missioned him, he has no reason to boast save concerning his weakness (12:5b–6). Such a boast is not foolish and far from arrogant. It does not elevate Paul above anyone else. It is truthful and humble (12:6).

In 12:7–9, Paul refers to "a thorn in his flesh"

which God gave him to prevent him from becoming
proud over his revelations. His reference to this thorn
is vague, and the text does not warrant a more precise
definition. Whatever it was, it proved extremely painful
to Paul and he had repeatedly pleaded for its removal.
However, he understood its divine purpose, which was
to reveal the power of grace. Paul thus boasts about his
weaknesses and about the insults, hardships, persecutions and agonies which he has suffered for Christ.
Since God reveals himself in Paul's weakness, that very
weakness is the source of his strength, so long as he
humbly confesses it (12:9-10).

STUDY QUESTIONS: Why does Paul refer to himself in
the third person in 12:2-5a? Is
there any difference between Paul's
visions and his revelations? How
does Paul see the purpose of his
weakness?

2 Corinthians 12:11–18
COMPARISON WITH THE ARCHAPOSTLES

11 I have been talking like a fool, but you forced me to do it: you are the ones who should have been commending me. Though I am a nobody, there is not a thing these archapostles have that 12 I do not have as well. ·You have seen done among you all the things that mark the true apostle, unfailingly produced: the signs, the 13 marvels, the miracles. ·Is there anything of which you have had less than the other churches have had, except that I have not myself been a burden on you? For this unfairness, please for- 14 give me. ·I am all prepared now to come to you for the third time, and I am not going to be a burden on you: it is you I want, not your pos- sessions. Children are not expected to save up 15 for their parents, but parents for children. ·I am perfectly willing to spend what I have, and to be expended, in the interests of your souls. Because I love you more, must I be loved the less? 16 All very well, you say: I personally put no pressure on you, but like the cunning fellow that 17 I am, I took you in by a trick. ·So we exploited you, did we, through one of the men that I have 18 sent to you? ·Well, Titus went at my urging, and I sent the brother that came with him. Can Titus have exploited you? You know that he and I have always been guided by the same spirit and trodden in the same tracks.

✠

By commending himself (11:30–33, 12:1–10), Paul has been talking like a fool (11:16–29). However, there should have been no need for him to do so (12:11). First of all, having everything which the archapostles have, he had amply demonstrated the marks of a true apostle (12:12). Second, the Corinthian community has received everything that the other churches have, with the exception of having to support Paul. Slipping into the tone of irony which characterized 11:16–21a, he apologizes for this deprivation (12:13).

Paul's economic independence and his willingness to rely on the community for sustenance (12:13b) is the subject of 12:14–15, where Paul announces his coming third visit to Corinth (see 2:1). Comparing himself to a parent, he reminds the Corinthians that it is not the children who must provide for the parents, but vice versa. Has not Paul expended everything he has for his children in Christ? Possessions are of no import. It is their souls which matter and which have been the object of Paul's ministry. By not depending on the Corinthians for support, he has actually shown that he loves them more. Why then should he be loved less?

Judging that by this time the Corinthians have been persuaded, he interprets their response and answers a fresh objection that he has tricked and exploited them. It is then he who would have played the role of the serpent and not the archapostles (12:16; see 11:3). Titus, whom Paul had sent to them and whom they loved, stands as living proof that this is not so (12:17–18).

STUDY QUESTIONS: What are the signs of a true apostle? What implications does Paul draw from the parent-child relationship?

2 Corinthians 12:19 – 13:13
TRAVEL PLANS, FINAL GREETINGS AND BLESSING

¹⁹ All this time you have been thinking that our defense is addressed to you, but it is before God that we, in Christ, are speaking; and it is all, my ²⁰ dear brothers, for your benefit. ·What I am afraid of is that when I come I may find you different from what I want you to be, and you may find that I am not as you would like me to be; and then there will be wrangling, jealousy, and tempers roused, intrigues and backbiting and gossip, ²¹ obstinacies and disorder. ·I am afraid that on my next visit, my God may make me ashamed on your account and I shall be grieving over all those who sinned before and have still not repented of the impurities, fornication and debauchery they committed.

¹ 13 This will be the third time I have come to you. The evidence of three, or at least two, witnesses is necessary to sustain the charge. ² I gave warning when I was with you the second time and I give warning now, too, before I come, to those who sinned before and to any others, that when I come again, I shall have no mercy. ³ You want proof, you say, that it is Christ speaking in me: you have known him not as a weak- ⁴ ling, but as a power among you? ·Yes, but he was crucified through weakness, and still he lives now through the power of God. So then, we are weak, as he was, but we shall live with him, through the power of God, for your benefit.

⁵ Examine yourselves to make sure you are in the faith; test yourselves. Do you acknowledge that Jesus Christ is really in you? If not, you have

⁶ failed the test, ·but we, as I hope you will come
⁷ to see, have not failed it. ·We pray to God that
you will do nothing wrong: not that we want to
appear as the ones who have been successful—we
would rather that you did well even though we
⁸ failed. ·We have no power to resist the truth; only
⁹ to further it. ·We are only too glad to be weak
provided you are strong. What we ask in our
¹⁰ prayers is for you to be made perfect. ·That is
why I am writing this from a distance, so that
when I am with you I shall not need to be strict,
with the authority which the Lord gave me for
building up and not for destroying.

¹¹   In the meantime, brothers, we wish you happiness; try to grow perfect; help one another. Be
united; live in peace, and the God of love and
peace will be with you.

¹²   Greet one another with the holy kiss. All the
saints send you greetings.

¹³   The grace of the Lord Jesus Christ, the love of
God and the fellowship of the Holy Spirit be with
you all.

✠

Paul's personal apologia (10:1 – 13:10) is now
brought to a close (12:19 – 13:10). This defense has
not been before the Corinthians but before God. The
reason that he addressed it to the Corinthians was that
they might benefit from it. Paul hopes that this purpose
has been fulfilled. If so, there should be no problems
between them and himself when he comes to Corinth.

Lingering fears do remain. Paul is not certain that
the sexual aberrations which had been of such concern
in 1 Corinthians and in his subsequent communication
with them have been eliminated (12:19–21). They had
been warned during his second visit, and they are now
being warned by the present letter. The time for warn-

ing, however, is coming to an end. On his coming third visit, Paul will reveal Christ's judging power (13:1–4).

The warning in 13:1–4 flows into an exhortation, prayer and further warnings (13:5–10). Paul's prayer is that the Corinthians be made perfect (13:9). He is writing in this way from a distance in the hope that problems will be resolved when he comes and that strictness will prove unnecessary. Paul's mission is similar to that of Jeremiah. However, whereas the latter was sent to destroy and to build (Jr 1:10), Paul's mission was not to destroy but to build up (13:10). So ends Paul's apologia.

The letter concludes with a series of brief exhortations, which summarize Paul's response to the community's many problems (13:11), some greetings, and a final blessing (13:12–13).

STUDY QUESTIONS: How is Paul's vocation related to that of the prophet Jeremiah? What is the relationship between the letter's concluding blessing and its opening greeting?

Philippians
The Letter of Paul
to the Christians of Philippi

INTRODUCTION

It is extremely difficult to define the precise situation which led to the writing of Philippians. Hypotheses for its date and place of origin also abound. The problem may well be that the letter which is now included in the New Testament was composed of several letters which Paul had written to the Philippians. Written on several occasions, the letters' internal evidence would necessarily prove conflicting for anyone who tried to find one particular date or occasion. In the commentary we have taken pains to point out the data which supports a multiple-letter theory.

For our purposes, however, it does not ultimately matter whether Philippians was originally more than one letter, perhaps even three, which were later edited. The fact is that as found in the New Testament and as received by the Church, the letter is now one, and we are invited to read it as such. The hypothetical letters which it includes may not all be complete. Given the elements which were retained and inserted in a new context, what we have is actually a new letter.

Two qualities stand out among all the others in the letter's view of Christianity: delicate gratitude (1:3–11, 4:10–20) and humility (2:1–11). As we read the letter we are especially thankful for the extraordinary Christian hymn which Paul quoted in 2:6–11. Through it we gain insight into the quality of the early Christian liturgy as well as into its influence on Christian reflection and ethical formation.

Philippians 1:1–11
ADDRESS AND THANKSGIVING

¹ **1** From Paul and Timothy, servants of Christ Jesus, to all the saints in Christ Jesus, together
² with their presiding elders and deacons. ·We wish you the grace and peace of God our Father and of the Lord Jesus Christ.

³ I thank my God whenever I think of you; and
⁴ every time I pray for all of you, I pray with joy,
⁵ remembering how you have helped to spread the Good News from the day you first heard it right
⁶ up to the present. ·I am quite certain that the One who began this good work in you will see that it is finished when the Day of Christ Jesus comes.
⁷ It is only natural that I should feel like this toward you all, since you have shared the privileges which have been mine: both my chains and my work defending and establishing the gospel. You
⁸ have a permanent place in my heart, ·and God knows how much I miss you all, loving you as
⁹ Christ Jesus loves you. ·My prayer is that your love for each other may increase more and more and never stop improving your knowledge and
¹⁰ deepening your perception ·so that you can always recognize what is best. This will help you to become pure and blameless, and prepare you for
¹¹ the Day of Christ, ·when you will reach the perfect goodness which Jesus Christ produces in us for the glory and praise of God.

✠

The letter to the church at Philippi opens with the customary form of address which had been developed for Christian apostolic letters (1:1–2). It continues with one of the most beautiful, personal and apostolically sensitive thanksgiving units which Paul wrote (1:3–11).

Its senders are Paul and Timothy (1:1). The latter had also been a co-sender of the letters to Thessalonika and 2 Corinthians, where he was described as "one of the brothers" (2 Co 1:1). In Philippians 1:1, he is introduced together with Paul as a servant of Christ Jesus. As we shall see, this development may be quite significant for the history of the letter. In Paul's other letters, the descriptive statements of Paul's Christian identity are always distinct from those of the co-senders.

The addressees are the saints in Christ Jesus who are at Philippi (1:1). The *Jerusalem Bible*'s omission of the location should be corrected with the insertion of "who are at Philippi" immediately after Christ Jesus. After this general reference to the saints, that is, to the members of the church, the letter adds "together with their presiding elders and deacons." The term which has been interpreted as "presiding elders" would be more literally translated as overseers or bishops. However, the latter were in fact elders, and their function was to preside over the church.

During Paul's life, it is unlikely that the overseers and deacons had already emerged as distinct and quasi-specialized roles or functions in the Church. We thus have evidence that the address may have been formulated at a later time. If indeed the present letter is an edited composite of several Pauline letters, the address could well have been written by the editor of Paul's Philippian correspondence. This position would accord with other data bearing on the historical development

of ministries in the life of the early Church. We would
also be able to appreciate the description of Timothy
as a servant along with Paul. With passing decades,
Timothy's place and significance in the Church's historical self-understanding became increasingly prominent.
Less a co-worker and associate, Timothy came to be
recognized and identified as one with Paul in the Gospel mission.

The thanksgiving unit (1:3–11) is remarkable for its
warmth and intimacy. Paul obviously felt very close to
the Philippians and he knew that they felt equally close
to him. In reading the unit, we sense none of the problems which made his relationship to Corinth so stormy.
Its tone of freedom and uninhibited communication
pervades the entire letter.

The unit begins with a report on Paul's attitude in
the present. His prayer of thanksgiving is for the way
the Philippians have helped in the Gospel mission from
the moment of their evangelization all the way to the
present (1:3–5). One of the ways they did this was by
sending Epaphroditus to assist Paul in his endeavors
(2:25). Paul's prayer is thus based on the community's
continuous history. However, it also looks to the future. The past provides secure grounds for hope that
the good work already begun will come to its comple-
tion on the day of Christ's return (1:6–7a). This hope
is also based on the present relationship of the Philippians to Paul and his Gospel service, a relationship
characterized by love (1:7b–8). Hope for the future is
thus based on historical faith, community solidarity
and love.

Concluding the unit, Paul affirms his prayer that the
Philippians continue to grow in love, knowledge, per-
ception and discernment (1:9). When Christ comes, he
will thus find them pure, blameless and perfect. It is

Christ himself who effects this goodness in them in
view of God's glory and praise (1:10–11). Through
his prayer, Paul also fulfills his prophetic mission to
console, encourage and build up the Christian life of
the community.

STUDY QUESTIONS: How does the address (1:1–2) support the hypothesis that Philippians
is a composite document? How is
Paul's thanksgiving unit related to
history and basic Christian attitudes?

Philippians 1:12–26
PAUL IN PRISON

¹² I am glad to tell you, brothers, that the things
that happened to me have actually been a help
to the Good News.

¹³ My chains, in Christ, have become famous not
¹⁴ only all over the Praetorium but everywhere, ·and
most of the brothers have taken courage in the
Lord from these chains of mine and are getting
more and more daring in announcing the Mes-
¹⁵ sage without any fear. ·It is true that some of
them are doing it just out of rivalry and competition, but the rest preach Christ with the right
¹⁶ intention, ·out of nothing but love, as they know
that this is my invariable way of defending the
¹⁷ gospel. ·The others, who proclaim Christ for jeal-
ous or selfish motives, do not mind if they make
¹⁸ my chains heavier to bear. ·But does it matter?
Whether from dishonest motives or in sincerity,
Christ is proclaimed; and that makes me happy;
¹⁹ and I shall continue being happy, because I know
this will help to save me, thanks to your prayers
and to the help which will be given to me by the
²⁰ Spirit of Jesus. ·My one hope and trust is that I
shall never have to admit defeat, but that now as
always I shall have the courage for Christ to be
glorified in my body, whether by my life or by
²¹ my death. ·Life to me, of course, is Christ, but
²² then death would bring me something more; ·but
then again, if living in this body means doing
work which is having good results—I do not know
²³ what I should choose. ·I am caught in this dilemma: I want to be gone and be with Christ,
²⁴ which would be very much the better, ·but for
me to stay alive in this body is a more urgent
²⁵ need for your sake. ·This weighs with me so

much that I feel sure I shall survive and stay with
you all, and help you to progress in the faith and
26 even increase your joy in it; ·and so you will have
another reason to give praise to Christ Jesus on
my account when I am with you again.

☩

The first part of the letter extends from 1:12 to 3:1.
It includes reflections on Paul's personal situation
(1:12–26), a warm exhortation to the Philippians
(1:27–2:18), and plans to send Timothy to them
along with the regrettable return to Philippi of
Epaphroditus, whom the Philippians had sent to assist
Paul (2:19–3:1). The concluding verse appears to
mark the end of the entire letter (3:1). It is especially
this verse and the sudden transition to verse 2 which
has convinced many scholars that the present letter to
the Philippians was composed of two or even three letters which originally had been quite distinct.

Paul's reference to his chains and to the Praetorium
(1:13) indicate that he is in prison at the time of writing. He had already referred to his imprisonment in the
thanksgiving unit (1:7). Reflecting on developments
all about him, Paul believes that his imprisonment has
actually worked for the spread of the gospel (1:12).

His imprisonment is well-known and has been a
source of courage among the brothers, who have taken
up the work of Christ in Paul's place. Not that all was
going absolutely smoothly. Motivations varied. There
were those who imitated Paul in preaching sincerely
and out of love, but there were also those who
preached out of a sense of rivalry, competition and
jealousy. These selfish motives are dishonest and reprehensible, but ultimately Paul recognizes that what mat-

ters above all is that Christ be proclaimed, little matter
that some are making his chains harder to bear
(1:13–18).

Rarely does Paul reflect so openly and extensively
on his personal situation and how it contributes to his
salvation (1:19–23). In spite of the dishonest motives
of some who have taken up his work, Paul is happy in
the knowledge that all he is experiencing will contribute to his salvation. In his support, he has the prayers
of the Philippians and the Spirit of Jesus. However, he
does recognize that these will not automatically be
effective. They require his courageous collaboration.
Paul's hope and trust is that he will have the courage to
accept Christ's glorification in his body, whether by
continuing to live or by dying. By living, Paul gives expression to the life of Christ; by dying, he would fulfill
Christ's promise of salvation for himself and for others.
Between the two, Paul is caught in a dilemma.

Paul's personal preference would be to die and be
with Christ. However, there are others to consider as
well as Paul's mission to them. For the sake of others,
then, Paul chooses life. This need is so great that Paul
is certain of survival. Even in his most personal reflections, Paul never loses sight of the mission to which he
has been called and of the communal good. Accordingly, even while in prison, he looks forward to being
once again with the Philippians. Progressing in the
faith, they will have even greater reason to praise Christ
Jesus because of what he has done on Paul's behalf
(1:23–26).

STUDY QUESTIONS: What values underlie Paul's reflec-
                 tions on his imprisonment? How
                 does he resolve the dilemma of
                 living or dying?

27 Avoid anything in your everyday lives that would be unworthy of the gospel of Christ, so that, whether I come to you and see for myself, or stay at a distance and only hear about you, I shall know that you are unanimous in meeting the attack with firm resistance, united by your
28 love for the faith of the gospel ·and quite unshaken by your enemies. This would be the sure sign that they will lose and you will be saved. It
29 would be a sign from God ·that he has given you the privilege not only of believing in Christ, but
30 of suffering for him as well. ·You and I are together in the same fight as you saw me fighting before and, as you will have heard, I am fighting still.

1 2 If our life in Christ means anything to you, if love can persuade at all, or the Spirit that we have in common, or any tenderness and sym-
2 pathy, ·then be united in your convictions and united in your love, with a common purpose and a common mind. That is the one thing which
3 would make me completely happy. ·There must be no competition among you, no conceit; but everybody is to be self-effacing. Always consider
4 the other person to be better than yourself, ·so that nobody thinks of his own interests first but everybody thinks of other people's interest in-
5 stead. ·In your minds you must be the same as Christ Jesus:

6 His state was divine,
yet he did not cling
to his equality with God
7 but emptied himself

to assume the condition of a slave,
and became as men are;
and being as all men are,
8   he was humbler yet,
even to accepting death,
death on a cross.
9   But God raised him high
and gave him the name
which is above all other names
10   so that all beings
in the heavens, on earth and in the underworld,
should bend the knee at the name of Jesus
11   and that every tongue should acclaim
Jesus Christ as Lord,
to the glory of God the Father.

12   So then, my dear friends, continue to do as I
tell you, as you always have; not only as you did
when I was there with you, but even more now
that I am no longer there; and work for your sal-
13   vation "in fear and trembling." ·It is God, for his
own loving purpose, who puts both the will and
14   the action into you. ·Do all that has to be done
15   without complaining or arguing ·and then you
will be innocent and genuine, perfect children of
God among a deceitful and underhand brood,
and you will shine in the world like bright stars
16   because you are offering it the word of life. This
would give me something to be proud of for the
Day of Christ, and would mean that I had not
run in the race and exhausted myself for nothing.
17   And then, if my blood has to be shed as part of
your own sacrifice and offering—which is your
faith—I shall still be happy and rejoice with all
18   of you, ·and you must be just as happy and rejoice with me.

✠

After presenting his own situation at the time of
writing (1:12–26), Paul turns to a warm and calm

exhortation, whose tone is nevertheless firm and demanding. The Philippians appear to have had few of the problems which troubled the Thessalonian and especially the Corinthian communities. Nor was Paul's authority challenged at Philippi. Accepted and loved by the Christians of the Roman colony, there was little danger that Paul's message would be misinterpreted. Consequently, there was no need for him to wrestle with questions of elementary morality. Nor did he have to defend his apostolic function or struggle to obviate distortions of his message. Writing to a community which was dedicated to the Gospel and warmly sympathetic to him, he exhorts its members to accept the challenge of Christian heroism (1:27–2:18).

Three aspects of the Christian ideal seemed most pertinent to the Philippian situation. First, Paul exhorts them to profess their faith firmly in all circumstances, but especially when others are distorting it (1:27–30). Second, he urges them to adopt the humility of Christ himself. In this they will find the key to creative harmony (2:1–11). Third and finally, he calls for the simple and straightforward way of life which befits children of God (2:12–18). These three areas of concern indicate that there were some problems at Philippi. Although these do not appear to have been severe, this was no cause for complacency. Everything which is inconsistent with the life of Christ must be eliminated from the lives of men and women who are bent on salvation (1:28, 2:12).

Paul's presence or absence should not affect the quality of Christian attitudes and behavior among the Philippians. In everything and at all times, the Gospel should be their norm (1:27). This is especially true when they and the Gospel are under attack. United in shared love for the faith, they shall then meet all such attacks with firm resistance (1:27). Unshaken, they will thus have a sign of their salvation as well as of their enemies' defeat (1:28). In addition, they will also have a sign that God has given them the privilege to suffer for the Gospel in which they believe (1:29). The Philippians are called to engage with Paul in the very fight which continues to take up his energies (1:30).

In his appeal for Gospel fidelity, Paul had emphasized the need for unity in a common effort (1:27). The same values underlie the second part of his exhortation. The Philippians must be united in their convictions, love, purpose and mind (2:2). To introduce and buttress his statement, Paul calls upon the life in Christ, the love, the common Spirit, the tenderness and the sympathy which he and the Philippians have been sharing with one another (2:1). The required unity precludes competition, conceit and self-interest, and is expressed in a self-effacing attitude which values others as better than oneself and seeks their interest (2:3-4). Such is the humility which is demonstrated in the mystery of Christ (2:5).

In 2:6-11, Paul then cites an early Christological hymn in which Christ's supreme act of humility leads to his divine glorification. In quoting this hymn, which demonstrates the extraordinary development of early Christology, faith experience and hymnology, Paul evokes the liturgical context in which it was sung and brings the whole force of Christian symbolic acts to bear on his exhortation. Unlike 1 Co 11:23-25 and 15:3-5, the traditional text is not quoted to prove or disprove anything or to demonstrate inconsistency in behavior or faith expression. Rather the hymn serves to articulate and shape the Christian attitude. It is in this context that the Scriptures and tradition serve their most basic and elevated function.

The structure, division and even the number of strophes in the Philippians' hymn are not clear, and many hypotheses have been presented to help Christians to appreciate the hymn's rich theology. For our purposes, it suffices to note that it includes two movements, Jesus Christ's self-emptying (*kenosis*) or humbling to the point of death (2:6–8), and God's subsequent act of glorification in which Jesus was exalted to a position which called for universal worship (2:9–11). In both sections, Paul may have added expressions which apply the hymn to the prose context of his letter and reflect elements of his own theology. Two such expressions may be "death on a cross" (2:8) and "in the heavens, on earth and in the underworld" (2:10).

The principal difficulty in the hymn's interpretation lies in its opening reference to Jesus' divine state and to his equality with God (2:6). Many have understood this as a reference to Jesus' preexistence, that is, to his life with God prior to the incarnation. The self-emptying (2:7) would thus be a reference to the incarnation, and this would represent an event distinct from Jesus' death on the cross (2:8). One of the main difficulties with such an interpretation is that it would presuppose an isolated and extremely early instance of belief in Jesus' preexistence. One wonders why this belief would not have influenced further theological reflection and left its mark on other New Testament works from this period. In view of the fact that the hymn was used in the liturgy, this ought to be expected.

We consequently propose that the hymn be interpreted otherwise, that is, as an expression of the Christian ideal which was realized in the historical life of Christ. This interpretation, which situates the hymn within early Christian thinking on Christ's relationship to Adam, reveals a work which was quite at home in the Christian world of Paul. It can best be presented by means of a paraphrase.

Like Adam or everyman, the state of Jesus Christ was divine, that is he was in the image and likeness of God. However, unlike Adam, he did not cling to his equality with God, reject his humanity and seek to be fully like God. Rather he accepted the human condition to be fully human, recognizing his relationship to God and God's absolute dominion. That human condition included death, and for Jesus this meant death on a cross (2:6–8). According to this interpretation, Jesus' radical humility would have been a fully adequate response to what would later be termed original sin.

Since Jesus had perfectly accepted his human status before God, God raised him and exalted his person and name above all others. Consequently, all must bend the knee before him in homage and acclaim him as Lord to the glory of God, the Father and source of his earthly and exalted life (2:9–11).

The exhortation concludes with a call to be perfect children of God (2:12–18). First, Paul recalls verse 1:27 by repeating that Christian behavior should not be affected by his presence or absence (2:12). As perfect children of God, they will shine like the stars (2:13–15). The ideal of perfection in human life and the glorification which ensues parallels the two parts of the hymn which Paul had just quoted and applied to the Philippians. If this is realized, Paul will rejoice that he has not run the Christian race in vain (2:16; see 1:30). Even if he has to suffer to the point of dying (2:17a; see 2:8 and 1:29), he will rejoice, and the Philippians must rejoice with him (2:17b–18).

STUDY QUESTIONS: What are two proposed interpretations of the hymn in 2:6–11? Which one is to be preferred? What reasons do you have for making this choice? What is the basic tone of Paul's exhortation? Why does it differ so sharply from exhortations in the Corinthian letters?

Philippians 2:19 – 3:1
REJOICE IN THE LORD

¹⁹ I hope, in the Lord Jesus, to send Timothy to you soon, and I shall be reassured by having news ²⁰ of you. ·I have nobody else like him here, as ²¹ wholeheartedly concerned for your welfare: ·all the rest seem more interested in themselves than ²² in Jesus Christ. ·But you know how he has proved himself by working with me on behalf of the ²³ Good News like a son helping his father. ·That is why he is the one that I am hoping to send you, as soon as I know something definite about my ²⁴ fate. ·But I continue to trust, in the Lord, that I shall be coming soon myself.

²⁵ It is essential, I think, to send brother Epaphroditus back to you. He was sent as your representative to help me when I needed someone to be my companion in working and battling, ²⁶ but he misses you all and is worried because you ²⁷ heard about his illness. ·It is true that he has been ill, and almost died, but God took pity on him, and on me as well as him, and spared me what ²⁸ would have been one grief on top of another. ·So I shall send him back as promptly as I can; you will be happy to see him again, and that will make ²⁹ me less sorry. ·Give him a most hearty welcome, in the Lord; people like him are to be honored. ³⁰ It was for Christ's work that he came so near to dying, and he risked his life to give me the help that you were not able to give me your-¹ 3 selves.

3 Finally, my brothers, rejoice in the Lord.

✠

The conclusion of this first part of Paul's letter to the Philippians deals with the mission of Timothy (2:19–24) and with Epaphroditus' return to Philippi (2:25–30). Its final line is an appeal to rejoice (3:1). It recalls the concluding words of Paul's exhortation, which asked the Philippians to join Paul in rejoicing (2:17–18). For the early Christians, rejoicing was the normal expression of a life lived in and with Christ for the salvation of others. Given the example of Christ, suffering did not inhibit such rejoicing. Since it led to a new and glorious life with God, it was rather a cause for rejoicing.

Timothy is with Paul, very likely at Ephesus, although the precise location from which this letter was written is not altogether clear. Paul is sending Timothy to Philippi. There can be no question of his credentials, since he has long been like a son to Paul and his only interest is in the Philippians' welfare (2:19–23). Even Timothy, however, cannot replace a personal visit from Paul, and the latter will come as soon as possible (2:24).

Epaphroditus had been sent by the church of Philippi to assist Paul in his difficult work. He had come as the community's representative. However, he had apparently taken ill and nearly died. Through God's mercy, he was still alive, but there was no point to his remaining with Paul. Besides, in his illness he had really missed the community that had sent him to Paul. Sensitive to these human realities, Paul therefore sends him back to Philippi. He is grateful for the service which he had already rendered but recognizes that a man should be with his own community (2:25–30). Even with the loss of Epaphroditus, Paul is able to rejoice and to ask the Philippians to rejoice with him (3:1).

STUDY QUESTIONS: How could suffering be a cause for
rejoicing? What relationship did
Epaphroditus have to the Philippians and to Paul?

Philippians 3:1 – 4:1
RACING FOR THE FINISH

¹ It is no trouble to me to repeat what I have already written to you, and as far as you are con- ² cerned, it will make for safety. ·Beware of dogs! Watch out for the people who are making mis- ³ chief. Watch out for the cutters. ·We are the real people of the circumcision, we who worship in accordance with the Spirit of God; we have our own glory from Christ Jesus without having to ⁴ rely on a physical operation. ·If it came to relying on physical evidence, I should be fully qualified myself. Take any man who thinks he can rely on what is physical: I am even better quali- ⁵ fied. ·I was born of the race of Israel and of the tribe of Benjamin, a Hebrew born of Hebrew parents, and I was circumcised when I was eight ⁶ days old. As for the Law, I was a Pharisee; ·as for working for religion, I was a persecutor of the Church; as far as the Law can make you per- ⁷ fect, I was faultless. ·But because of Christ, I have come to consider all these advantages that ⁸ I had as disadvantages. ·Not only that, but I believe nothing can happen that will outweigh the supreme advantage of knowing Christ Jesus my Lord. For him I have accepted the loss of everything, and I look on everything as so much rub- ⁹ bish if only I can have Christ ·and be given a place in him. I am no longer trying for perfection by my own efforts, the perfection that comes from the Law, but I want only the perfection that comes through faith in Christ, and is from ¹⁰ God and based on faith. ·All I want is to know Christ and the power of his resurrection and to share his sufferings by reproducing the pattern

¹¹ of his death. ·That is the way I can hope to take
¹² my place in the resurrection of the dead. ·Not
that I have become perfect yet: I have not yet
won, but I am still running, trying to capture the
¹³ prize for which Christ Jesus captured me. ·I can
assure you my brothers, I am far from thinking
that I have already won. All I can say is that I
forget the past and I strain ahead for what is still
¹⁴ to come; ·I am racing for the finish, for the prize
to which God calls us upward to receive in Christ
¹⁵ Jesus. ·We who are called "perfect" must all think
in this way. If there is some point on which you
see things differently, God will make it clear to
¹⁶ you; ·meanwhile, let us go forward on the road
that has brought us to where we are.
¹⁷   My brothers, be united in following my rule of
life. Take as your models everybody who is already doing this and study them as you used to
¹⁸ study us. ·I have told you often, and I repeat it
today with tears, there are many who are behav-
¹⁹ ing as the enemies of the cross of Christ. ·They
are destined to be lost. They make foods into
their god and they are proudest of something
they ought to think shameful; the things they
²⁰ think important are earthly things. ·For us, our
homeland is in heaven, and from heaven comes
the Savior we are waiting for, the Lord Jesus
²¹ Christ, ·and he will transfigure these wretched
bodies of ours into copies of his glorious body.
He will do that by the same power with which he
can subdue the whole universe.

¹4 So then, my brothers and dear friends, do not
give way but remain faithful in the Lord. I
miss you very much, dear friends; you are my joy
and my crown.

✠

There can be no denying the extremely sharp change
in attitude from 1:27 – 3:1 to 3:2 – 4:1. In the former

section, the impression was given that there were few problems at Philippi. Now Paul is extremely concerned about many people who are threatening the community's fidelity to the Gospel. The main problem stems from pressure to return to Jewish observances and the circumcision (3:3). We are reminded of the situation which drew Paul's harsh response in the letter to the Galatians (3:1–5).

Paul now argues that Judaism and the physical circumcision are of no account, now that Christ is risen. In 3:5–6, we have some precious information on Paul's personal background as an Israelite of the tribe of Benjamin who was born of Hebrew parents and who had been a Pharisee, a persecutor of Christians and one perfect before the Law. In relation to knowing Christ the Lord, however, all of these things are of no account (3:7–9). All that matters is that Paul reproduce the pattern of Christ's death in order to share in his resurrection (3:10–11). At present his life is like a race to the finish and its goal is Christ himself. The Philippians must join him en route (3:12–16).

In 3:17–21, Paul exhorts the Philippians to follow his rule of life and to imitate those who do so. The principle of imitation, which in some form is found in all Paul's letters, applies not to Paul alone but to all Christians who are faithful in the Lord (4:1).

STUDY QUESTIONS: What does this section teach us about Paul's background? On what basis does Paul argue that the circumcision, Jewish observances and even being Jewish is no longer of any account?

Philippians 4:2–9
FINAL APPEALS

2   I appeal to Evodia and I appeal to Syntyche to
    come to agreement with each other, in the Lord;
3   and I ask you, Syzygus, to be truly a "compan-
    ion" and to help them in this. These women were
    a help to me when I was fighting to defend the
    Good News—and so, at the same time, were
    Clement and the others who worked with me.
    Their names are written in the book of life.
4   I want you to be happy, always happy in the
    Lord; I repeat, what I want is your happiness.
5   Let your tolerance be evident to everyone: the
6   Lord is very near. ·There is no need to worry;
    but if there is anything you need, pray for it, ask-
7   ing God for it with prayer and thanksgiving, ·and
    that peace of God, which is so much greater than
    we can understand, will guard your hearts and
8   your thoughts, in Christ Jesus. ·Finally, brothers,
    fill your minds with everything that is true, every-
    thing that is noble, everything that is good and
    pure, everything that we love and honor, and ev-
    erything that can be thought virtuous or worthy
9   of praise. ·Keep doing all the things that you
    learned from me and have been taught by me and
    have heard or seen that I do. Then the God of
    peace will be with you.

✠

The passage begins with an appeal to certain
members of the community to agree among themselves
(4:2–3). It is unclear how this unit is related to the

history of Paul's correspondence with Philippi. Within
the present form of the letter, however, it accords
well with the appeal for harmony which underlies
1:27 – 2:18. In that unit, Paul had exhorted the community on three points, and the second of these
(2:1–11) had included teaching on humility as the
basis for Christian harmony. In 4:2–3, we thus have
particular relationships which could well have called
for such teaching.

Following the appeal to Evodia, Syntyche and Syzygus (4:2–3), Paul moves into an exhortation of a
fairly general nature (4:4–9). The Philippians must be
happy, tolerant, without worry and prayerful. The
Lord is near, and they shall soon enjoy God's peace.

STUDY QUESTIONS: How is this unit related to the rest
of the letter? How is Paul's exhor-
tation related to expectations of
Christ's coming?

Philippians 4:10–23
FINAL THANKSGIVING AND GREETINGS

10 It is a great joy to me, in the Lord, that at last you have shown some concern for me again; though of course you were concerned before, and

11 only lacked an opportunity. ·I am not talking about shortage of money: I have learned to man-

12 age on whatever I have, ·I know how to be poor and I know how to be rich too. I have been through my initiation and now I am ready for anything anywhere: full stomach or empty stom-

13 ach, poverty or plenty. ·There is nothing I can-not master with the help of the One who gives

14 me strength. ·All the same, it was good of you to

15 share with me in my hardships. ·In the early days of the Good News, as you people of Philippi well know, when I left Macedonia, no other church helped me with gifts of money. You were the only

16 ones; ·and twice since my stay in Thessalonika

17 you have sent me what I needed. ·It is not your gift that I value; what is valuable to me is the interest that is mounting up in your account.

18 Now for the time being I have everything that I need and more: I am fully provided now that I have received from Epaphroditus the offering that you sent, a sweet fragrance—the sacrifice that God

19 accepts and finds pleasing. ·In return my God will fulfill all your needs, in Christ Jesus, as lavishly

20 as only God can. ·Glory to God, our Father, for ever and ever. Amen.

21 My greetings to every one of the saints in Christ Jesus. The brothers who are with me send their

22 greetings. ·All the saints send their greetings, es-

23 pecially those of the imperial household. ·May

the grace of the Lord Jesus Christ be with your
spirit.

✠

Paul's final thanksgiving (4:10–20) might well have
represented yet a third letter to Philippi, or at least a
part of such a letter. The apostle's attitude in these
verses is very different from that found in 3:2–4:9,
and the reference to Epaphroditus (4:18) presupposes
that he has just arrived with help from Philippi and not
that he is about to leave Paul after a severe illness
(2:25–30). The main point of the unit is thanksgiving
for the assistance which the Philippians have sent via
Epaphroditus.

Within Philippians' present form, the unit tempers
the harsher statements found especially in 3:2–4:1.
From a structural point of view, it corresponds to the
thanksgiving unit given in the introduction (1:3–11).
The letter thus begins and ends with greetings (1:1–2,
4:21–23) and with thanksgiving (1:3–9, 4:10–20).

The passage is particularly rich with details on how
Paul has learned to manage in difficult situations as
well as with historical information. It presupposes that
Paul has had regular communication with the Philippians after his brief stay in that city upon first coming
to Macedonia. Paul refers to his work in Thessalonika
and the way the Philippians had twice come to his aid
since then. The letter he now writes expresses gratitude
for a third gift brought by Epaphroditus (4:15–20).

In 4:17, money and interest provide a metaphor for
salvation. The Philippians' gift is drawing interest
which is accumulating in their account. Their gift is

thus banked for their own ultimate benefit, and God
will fill their needs accordingly (4:19).

The letter concludes with greetings and a prayer of
blessing (4:21–23). The reference to the imperial
household does not necessarily refer to Rome. Like the
praetorian guard (1:13) it could refer to any Roman
administrative center. All that can be concluded with
certitude is that Paul is writing from a Roman capital.

STUDY QUESTIONS: What evidence do we have that
4:10–20 might refer to a distinct
letter of Paul? How does Paul use
financial dealings as a metaphor for
Christian life? Does the reference to
the imperial household necessarily
point to a Roman origin for the
letter?

Philemon
The Letter from Paul to Philemon

INTRODUCTION

The letter to Philemon is the shortest of the Pauline letters and one of four (the others, 1 and 2 Timothy, Titus) which were written to individuals. The other three, however, focus primarily on the ministerial challenge of the addresses, and the author never loses sight of the churches which they are called to lead. By contrast, Philemon is delicately personal.

Bringing to bear all the arguments which stem from his personal relationship to both Philemon and a runaway slave, whom Paul is sending back to him, we find Paul here at his persuasive best. We can hardly imagine that Philemon could have turned down Paul's request. In reading it, we are invited to join Paul in his use of rhetoric and psychology in the service of the Gospel.

1 From Paul, a prisoner of Christ Jesus and from our brother Timothy; to our dear fellow worker 2 Philemon, ·our sister Apphia, our fellow soldier Archippus and the church that meets in your 3 house; ·wishing you the grace and the peace of God our Father and the Lord Jesus Christ.

4 I always mention you in my prayers and thank 5 God for you, ·because I hear of the love and the faith which you have for the Lord Jesus and for 6 all the saints. ·I pray that this faith will give rise to a sense of fellowship that will show you all the 7 good things that we are able to do for Christ. ·I am so delighted, and comforted, to know of your love; they tell me, brother, how you have put new heart into the saints.

8 Now, although in Christ I can have no diffidence about telling you to do whatever is your 9 duty, ·I am appealing to your love instead, reminding you that this is Paul writing, an old man now and, what is more, still a prisoner of Christ 10 Jesus. ·I am appealing to you for a child of mine, whose father I became while wearing these chains: 11 I mean Onesimus. ·He was of no use to you before, but he will be useful to you now, as he has 12 been to me. ·I am sending him back to you, and 13 with him—I could say—a part of my own self. ·I should have liked to keep him with me; he could have been a substitute for you, to help me while I am in the chains that the Good News has brought 14 me. ·However, I did not want to do anything without your consent; it would have been forcing your 15 act of kindness, which should be spontaneous. ·I know you have been deprived of Onesimus for a

time, but it was only so that you could have him
¹⁶ back for ever, ·not as a slave any more, but something much better than a slave, a dear brother; especially dear to me, but how much more to you,
as a blood brother as well as a brother in the
¹⁷ Lord. ·So if all that we have in common means
anything to you, welcome him as you would me;
¹⁸ but if he has wronged you in any way or owes you
¹⁹ anything, then let me pay for it. ·I am writing this
in my own handwriting: I, Paul, shall pay it back
—I will not add any mention of your own debt to
²⁰ me, which is yourself. ·Well then, brother, I am
counting on you, in the Lord; put new heart into
²¹ me, in Christ. ·I am writing with complete confidence in your compliance, sure that you will do
even more than I ask.
²²   There is another thing: will you get a place
ready for me to stay in? I am hoping through
your prayers to be restored to you.
²³   Epaphras, a prisoner with me in Christ Jesus,
²⁴ sends his greetings; ·so do my colleagues Mark,
Aristarchus, Demas and Luke.
²⁵   May the grace of our Lord Jesus Christ be with
your spirit.

✠

The letter to Philemon is a short personal document,
written with loving astuteness to persuade the addressee to welcome a runaway slave whom Paul is now
sending back. From the names mentioned in the address (1–3) and the conclusion (23–24), Philemon
must have been a resident of Colossae (Col 4:7–17).
   The letter is actually addressed to several individuals, and Paul is mindful of the church that meets in
Philemon's house. The early Christians used to gather
for their weekly assembly in the home of one of their
leaders. Philemon would thus have been the head of a

house-church. As in 1 and 2 Thessalonians, 2 Corinthians and Philippians, Timothy is named as a co-sender of the letter (1–3).

The letter seems to have been written while Paul was a prisoner (1,9–10), unless he is speaking figuratively, which is not very probable. If the letter was written around the same time as Colossians, it would very likely have been sent from Rome around the year A.D. 62.

After the greeting, Paul includes a brief thanksgiving unit as had become his custom. Characteristically, Paul uses the thanksgiving to prepare the reader for the main message. In this case he emphasizes Philemon's sense of fellowship and his love for Paul (4–7). Love will be the basis for accepting Paul's special request, and fellowship will move him to integrate Onesimus, the runaway slave, into his household.

In the body of the letter (8–21), Paul begins by appealing to Philemon's love for him, a love that should be fanned by Paul's status as a prisoner and his old age (8–9). His request has to do with one who has become his child in Christ. While in prison, Paul consequently had considerable freedom to continue his work of evangelization. Since Paul is Onesimus' father in a sense, he has the life of Paul within him, so that as he returns to Colossae he in fact brings Paul with him (10–12). Actually, Paul would very much have liked to keep Onesimus with himself in Rome. Through the latter, Philemon would have been present to Paul, just as Paul would now be present to Philemon (13). However, Paul would not have wanted to infringe Philemon's rights. Consent must be spontaneous (14–15).

This first part of the body of the letter (8–15) has very carefully prepared the second by disposing Philemon to accept Paul's request. The latter is given in the second part (16–21).

Onesimus' name means "useful." In his request that Philemon receive Onesimus no longer as a slave but as a brother in the Lord (15–17) Paul knows that actually Onesimus had been of no use to Philemon up until now, in comparison with how useful he would now be (11). If Onesimus owes Philemon anything, Paul himself will pay (18), but Philemon should not forget his own Christian debt to Paul (19).

In the conclusion, Paul announces that in spite of his imprisonment, he still hopes to be able to visit Philemon and would like to enjoy his hospitality (22). Among those who send greetings, we should note Mark and Luke, whose names were to become even more prominent as the writers of two of our Gospel narratives.

STUDY QUESTIONS: What techniques of persuasion does Paul use in writing to Philemon? What does the letter contribute to our historical understanding of Paul? What is the basis for associating Philemon with Colossae?

SUGGESTED READINGS

Bartlett, David L. *Paul's Vision for the Teaching Church*. Valley Forge, Pa.: Judson, 1977. This book studies the implications of Paul's theology for understanding the teaching mission of the Church.

Beare, Frank W. *St. Paul and His Letters*. Nashville: Abingdon, 1962. A very readable set of essays on Paul and his letters in relation to their historical context.

Giblin, Charles H. *In Hope of God's Glory*. New York: Herder and Herder, 1970. A study of the text of Paul's letters with special focus on his theology. This work is especially useful after reading a more general work.

Käsemann, Ernst. *Jesus Means Freedom*. Philadelphia: Fortress, 1972. While the scope of this work is broader than Paul's letters, it helps to situate Paul's theology in the general context of the entire New Testament.

Keck, Leander E. *Paul and His Letters*. Philadelphia: Fortress, 1979. An excellent study of Paul, his Gospel and the fundamental themes and issues developed in his letters.

Meeks, Wayne A. *The Writings of St. Paul*. New York: W. W. Norton, 1972. A well-annotated text of Paul's undisputed letters together with a collection of valuable writings and articles from various historical periods.

Nock, Arthur Darby. *St. Paul*. New York: Harper & Row, 1963. A classic work, first published in 1938, on St. Paul, his letters, their style and their thought. The author is especially sensitive to the world of Paul.

Scroggs, Robin. *Paul for a New Day*. Philadelphia: Fortress, 1977. This work presupposes a good introduction to Paul and means to explore the existential nature of his thought in relation especially to psychological and sociological models and insights.

Stanley, David M. *Boasting in the Lord*. New York: Paulist, 1973. This is an excellent and comprehensive study of the phenomenon of prayer in the writings of St. Paul.

Stendahl, Krister. *Paul among Jews and Gentiles*. Philadelphia: Fortress, 1976. Many basic insights and reflections on how Paul has been approached are included in this study of Paul's views and efforts with regard to the relationship between Jews and Gentiles.

Taylor, Michael J., ed. *A Companion to Paul*. New York: Alba, 1975. An excellent collection of articles which have been found extremely useful for the study of Paul's theology.